图说中国梦V
The Chinese Dream in Pictures
Series V

运河文物

CULTURAL HERITAGE OF CHINA'S GRAND CANAL

中国新闻图片网　主编
Compiled by CNSphoto.com

First Edition 2024

Compiled By CNSphoto.com
Translated by Liu Yang
Book Design by He Yuting

ISBN 978-7-5104-8032-4

Published by
NEW WORLD PRESS
24 Baiwanzhuang Street, Beijing 100037, China

Distributed by
NEW WORLD PRESS
24 Baiwanzhuang Street, Beijing 100037, China
Tel: 86-10-68995968
Fax: 86-10-68998705
Website: www.nwp.com.cn
E-mail: nwpcd@sina.com

Printed in the People's Republic of China

中国大运河示意图
Route of China's Grand Canal

隋唐大运河
The Sui-Tang Grand Canal

京杭大运河对隋唐大运河截弯取直
The Beijing-Hangzhou Grand Canal was formed from the reconstructed and straightened Sui-Tang Grand Canal

浙东运河
The East Zhejiang Canal

前言

中国大运河由京杭大运河、隋唐大运河、浙东运河三部分构成，跨越了2500多年历史，绵延近3200公里，从北至南流经北京、天津、河北、山东、河南、安徽、江苏、浙江8个省和直辖市，串联起钱塘江、长江、淮河、黄河、海河五大水系。

中国大运河，如中华大地之血脉，滋养着泱泱华夏，见证着历代千秋、千年文明。

Preface

The Grand Canal in China spans more than 2,500 years of history and stretches for nearly 3,200 kilometers, connecting five major river systems – the Haihe River, the Yellow River, the Huaihe River, the Yangtze River, and the Qiantang River. From north to south, it flows through eight municipalities and provinces – Beijing, Tianjin, Hebei, Shandong, Henan, Anhui, Jiangsu, and Zhejiang, and can be divided into three segments – the Beijing-Hangzhou Grand Canal, the Sui-Tang Grand Canal, and the East Zhejiang Canal.

It is the lifeblood of China's vast land, nourishing the nation and witnessing the evolution of its time-honored civilization.

运：通济南北 联通古今

Canal Transport: Connecting the South and North, and the Past and Present

一条大运河，半部华夏史。

中国大运河肇始于春秋时期开凿的连接长江和淮河的人工渠道——邗沟。秦、汉、魏、晋和南北朝时期继续开凿延伸河道。

隋代，为贯通黄河、淮河与长江水系，促进南北文化交流和经济发展，开凿了永济渠、通济渠和江南运河，重新疏通邗沟，形成以洛阳为中心、北至涿郡（今北京）、南达余杭（今杭州）的隋唐大运河。

隋唐大运河在唐代、北宋得到进一步开凿、疏浚、整修。此后，由于黄河多次改道和淤积，隋唐大运河运输效率降低， 永济渠、通济渠逐渐失修而湮废。如今，隋唐大运河不再作为交通要道使用，但其历史遗迹和部分河段仍然存在，仍发挥着文化和水利方面的作用。

元代，开凿了济州河、会通河和通惠河，对隋唐大运河进行改造，截弯取直，形成了京杭大运河。其在明清时期经过多次疏浚和治理，成为南北交通和漕运要道。京杭大运河是世界上里程最长、工程最大的古代运河，至今仍发挥着重要交通和水利功能。

The Grand Canal has witnessed half of China's history.

It originates from Hangou, a canal dug in the Spring and Autumn Period (770-476 BC) to connect the Yangtze and Huaihe rivers. The canal was further excavated and extended during a succession of dynasties – Qin (221-206 BC), Han (206 BC-AD 220), the Three Kindoms period (220-280), Jin (265-420), and the Southern and Northern Dynasties (420-589).

In the Sui Dynasty (581-618), in order to connect the Yellow River, the Huaihe River, and the Yangtze River and to promote cultural exchanges between the south and the north and their economic development, three canals were constructed – Yongji, Tongji, and Jiangnan. The Hangou Canal was reopened, and the Sui-Tang Grand Canal was formed, with the city of Luoyang as its center and extending to Zhuojun (now Beijing) in the north and Yuhang (now Hangzhou) in the south.

The Sui-Tang Grand Canal was further excavated, dredged, and renovated in the Tang (618-907) and Northern Song (960-1127) dynasties. Then due to repeated diversion and siltation of the Yellow River, the transport efficiency of the canal dropped, and the Yongji Canal and the Tongji Canal gradually fell into disrepair and were abandoned. Today, the Sui-Tang Grand Canal is no longer a major transport route, but its historical sites have given it a role in culture, and the surviving sections still have water conservancy functions.

In the Yuan Dynasty (1206-1368), three more rivers were dug – Jizhou, Huitong, and Tonghui, and the Sui-Tang Grand Canal was reconstructed and straightened to form the Beijing-Hangzhou Grand Canal. It was dredged and managed many times in the Ming (1368-1644) and Qing (1616-1911) dynasties, and became an important route for north-south traffic and canal transport. The Beijing-Hangzhou Grand Canal is the longest and largest ancient canal in

浙东运河与京杭大运河南端相连，呈东南走向，西起杭州，东至宁波入海。其历史可追溯至春秋战国时期开凿的山阴故水道，最初用于挡潮、排涝和农田灌溉，后逐渐发展为重要的航运通道。南宋时，物资可经由这条运河开启海上丝绸之路。浙东运河至今仍发挥着重要的水利、航运和生态作用。

2014 年，在第三十八届世界遗产大会上，中国大运河作为文化遗产正式列入世界遗产名录，其中包含河道遗产 27 段，总长度 1011 公里；古桥、古纤道、盐商故居、历史街区等遗产共 58 处。联合国教科文组织世界遗产委员会认为，大运河是世界上最长的、最古老的人工水道，也是工业革命前规模最大、范围最广的土木工程项目，它促进了中国南北物资的交流和领土的统一管辖，反映出中国人民高超的智慧、决心和勇气，以及东方文明在水利技术和管理能力方面的杰出成就。

the world, and still plays an important role in water transport and water conservancy.

The East Zhejiang Canal is connected to the southern end of the Beijing-Hangzhou Grand Canal. It runs southeast from Hangzhou in the west to Ningbo in the east. Its history dates back to an ancient waterway dug in Shaoxing during the Spring and Autumn Period and the Warring States Period (475-221 BC). It was originally used to block tides, and for drainage and farmland irrigation, and then gradually developed into an important shipping channel. In the Southern Song Dynasty (1127-1279), goods were sent to the Maritime Silk Road via this canal. The East Zhejiang Canal still plays an important role in water conservancy, shipping, and eco-environmental conservation.

China's Grand Canal was officially listed on the UNESCO World Heritage List at the 38th session of the World Heritage Committee in 2014. The World Heritage Committee announced that the Grand Canal is the longest and oldest artificial waterway in the world, and also the largest and most extensive civil engineering project before the Industrial Revolution. It has not only fostered the exchange of goods between the north and south of China and the unification of the territory, but also reflects the wisdom, determination, and courage of the Chinese people and the outstanding achievements of the Chinese civilization in water conservancy technology. Twenty-seven riverway sections with a total length of 1,011 kilometers are included in the honor, as well as 58 heritage sites such as ancient bridges, towpaths, residences of salt merchants, and historical streets.

蕴：文脉赓续 泽被千秋

Canal Culture: A Legacy through Ages

运河泽两岸，水脉通文脉。

中国大运河拥有河道、古建筑、古遗址、石刻等各级各类遗存逾1200处，水工设施等重要代表性遗存368处，沿线集聚了国家级非物质文化遗产450多项。

大运河的河道开凿、水利工程设计与大自然的鬼斧神工相得益彰。

大运河沿线点缀着独具韵味的古桥古塔、亭台楼阁、中式园林、会馆庙宇。

大运河促进了南北交流和贸易往来，扬州盐运、淮安漕运随着大运河发展而兴盛，沿岸码头渔村由小壮大，蓬勃发展成水乡古镇和运河城市。

大运河文化与京津文化、燕赵文化、齐鲁文化、中原文化、吴越文化交汇碰撞，衍生出戏曲、武术、书画、庙会等丰富多彩的非物质文化遗产。

大运河的开凿和沿线的繁荣反映出中国人敢为人先、敢于创新的精神，开放包容、兼收并蓄的胸怀……

The Grand Canal has nourished its banks and given rise to a magnificent culture.

It boasts more than 1,200 relics of various levels and kinds, including waterways, ancient buildings, ruins, and stone carvings, and 368 important representative sites including water conservancy facilities, and more than 450 items of national intangible cultural heritage along its route.

The excavated waterways and water conservancy projects complement the wonders of nature.

The Grand Canal is also dotted with unique ancient bridges, pagodas, pavilions, classical gardens, guild halls, and temples.

It promoted trade and exchanges between the north and south of China. Salt transport in Yangzhou and canal transport in Huai'an both flourished with the development of the Grand Canal. The small fishing villages along the route grew into large water towns and canal cities.

The Grand Canal culture merged and collided with the Beijing-Tianjin culture, the Yan-Zhao culture of Hebei, the Qi-Lu culture of Shandong, the Central Plains culture in Henan, and the Wu-Yue culture in Jiangsu and Zhejiang, giving birth to a diverse range of intangible cultural heritage such as traditional operas, martial arts, calligraphy, painting, and temple fairs.

The construction of the Grand Canal reflects the creativity and pioneering spirit of the Chinese people, and the prosperity along the route exhibits their open and inclusive vision.

目录

CONTENTS

北京
一枝塔影认通州

1

Beijing
Tongzhou Viewed Against Its Backdrop Tower

“云光水色潞河秋，满径槐花感旧游。无恙蒲帆新雨后，一枝塔影认通州。”循着清代诗人王维珍（1827—1884）唯美的诗句，碧水潋滟的大运河北京段跃然于眼前，古塔凌云、帆樯林立、客商往来的一幕幕仿佛就在昨日。

大运河北京段流经昌平、海淀、西城、东城、朝阳、顺义、通州7个区。沿线有河道、水源、水利工程设施（闸）、航运工程设施（桥梁、码头）、古代运河设施和管理机构遗存（仓库）、古遗址、古建筑、石刻等物质文化遗产。

从“龙泉漱玉”的白浮泉到“银锭观山”的什刹海，从“拱卫京师”的永通桥到“一枝塔影”的燃灯塔，再到“五河交汇”的通州运河，沿线文物等级高、分布密集、时代跨度长、类型丰富，汇聚众多人文遗迹和自然景观。还有像“通州运河船工号子”这样的非物质文化遗产。

这些文化遗产彰显出气势恢宏的古都底蕴和古往今来的历史人文特色。

“Clouds cast their shadow on the water of the beautiful Luhe River in the fall. The path is strewn with locust flowers, which reminds me of my visit in the past. Standing on the firm boat built of rushes after fresh rain, I recognize Tongzhou from the reflection of its tower.” This beautiful poem by Qing Dynasty poet Wang Weizhen (1827-1884) vividly evokes the beautiful scenery of the Grand Canal with its clear water passing through Beijing, and the past scenes of ancient pagodas, sailing ships, and merchants bustling to and fro seem to have happened just yesterday.

The Beijing section of the Grand Canal flows through seven districts: Changping, Haidian, Xicheng, Dongcheng, Chaoyang, Shunyi, and Tongzhou. The cultural heritage along the route includes the remnants of ancient water conservancy engineering such as canals and sluices, shipping facilities like bridges and docks, and management agencies like warehouses. In addition, there are relics of tangible cultural heritage such as ancient ruins, buildings, and stone carvings.

From the gurgling Baifu Spring to the Yinding Bridge (Silver Ingot Bridge) at Shichahai with its spectacular hillside view, from the Yongtong Bridge that “defended” the ancient capital to the majestic Randeng Pagoda with its lighthouse, and then to the Tongzhou Canal where five rivers meet – these iconic cultural relics along the canal represent a long time span and a rich diversity, as well as different natural landscapes. There is also an abundance of intangible cultural heritage along the route, embodied by the traditional Tongzhou Canal boatmen’s songs.

These milestones show the magnificent heritage of the ancient capital as well as the historical and cultural characteristics of both the past and present.

白浮之泉
白浮泉遗址

白浮泉遗址处，人们在庭阁中乘凉。白浮泉遗址位于北京市昌平区龙山，是通惠河的水源地，建有九龙池和都龙王庙。九龙池得名于流水出处的九个青石雕刻的龙头。“九龙池”吐出清水的“龙泉漱玉”盛景是昌平八景之一。

在元代，水利专家郭守敬主持开凿了元大都都城至通州间的漕路——通惠河。为了引水济漕，他上奏元世祖忽必烈引白浮泉水作大运河北端上游水源，以瓮山泊（今颐和园昆明湖）为济运水库，以积水潭（今什刹海）为最终停泊港。图 / 李志明

Visitors enjoy the cool air in the Baifu Spring pavilion. The spring, located at the foot of Longshan Mountain in Changping District, Beijing, is the source of the Tonghui River. The pond built at the site is named the Jiulong Pond (Nine-Dragon Pond), after its nine dragonhead-shaped limestone faucets. The sound made by the water gushing out of the faucets is fancifully imagined to resemble dragons spitting out with jade in their mouths, and the site is regarded as one of the eight great scenic spots in Changping. The Du Dragon-King Temple is also located here.

In the Yuan Dynasty, Guo Shoujing (1231-1316), a water conservancy engineer, was given the task of building a waterway between Beijing, which was the capital city, and Tongzhou. Guo ordered a canal to be dug, which became known as the Tonghui River. He planned to divert water to it from the Baifu Spring, which became the upstream water source at the northern end of the Grand Canal. Guo also built the Wengshanbo reservoir (now Kunming Lake in the Summer Palace) and Jishuitan Lake (now Shichahai) to keep the water level in the canal stable. Jishuitan Lake was the final port of call. Guo had to report to Yuan Emperor Kublai Khan (1215-1294) and obtain permission for the work. Photograph by Li Zhiming

白浮泉遗址出土的石制构件，摆放在龙山之巅的都龙王庙院内。图 / 富田

Stone relics excavated from the Baifu Spring site stand guard before the Du Dragon-King Temple on Longshan Mountain. Photograph by Fu Tian

颐和园昆明湖上的绣漪桥，始建于清乾隆年间，是长河与昆明湖的水路交通要道。

清代，因白浮泉水至瓮山泊的水道堰塞，乾隆皇帝梳理香山、玉泉山一带泉脉水道，拓展昆明湖，这一做法解决了西郊水患，同时为城市供水、农田灌溉、漕运以及园林建设提供了充沛的优质水源，最终形成玉泉山－玉河－昆明湖－长河－护城河－通惠河－大运河这一立体水系。图 / 石艺媛

The Xiuyi Bridge over Kunming Lake in the Summer Palace. Built during Emperor Qianlong's reign (1736-1796), the fourth emperor of the Qing Dynasty, it was a major transport link between Kunming Lake and the Changhe River.

During the Qing Dynasty, the waterway from Baifu Spring to Wengshanbo became blocked. Emperor Qianlong ordered the spring waterways in the Fragrant Hills (Xiaingshan) and Yuquan Mountain to be dredged and had Kunming Lake expanded. This measure addressed the flood problem in the western suburbs, and also provided abundant high-quality water for urban areas, farmland irrigation, canal transport, and the construction of classical gardens. Eventually, a three-dimensional water system was formed consisting of the Yuquan Mountain, the Yuhe, Changhe and Tonghui rivers, the moat surrounding the ancient city wall, Kunming Lake, and the Grand Canal. Photograph by Shi Yiyuan

颐和园昆明湖，位于北京市海淀区。图 / 张炜

Kunming Lake in the Summer Palace, Haidian District, Beijing. Photograph by Zhang Wei

广源闸今貌以及新修复的龙王庙。

广源闸，位于北京市海淀区，建于元代，元通惠河二十四闸之一，是长河上保存最完好的桥闸。图 / 石艺媛

The Guangyuan sluice and the newly restored Dragon-King Temple.

The Guangyuan sluice, located in Haidian District, Beijing, is one of the 24 sluices of the Tonghui River. Photograph by Shi Yiyuan

万寿寺，位于北京市海淀区，历经明清两朝兴修、扩建，形成了集寺院、园林、皇家行宫于一体的大型古代建筑群，是自昆明湖向东、长河沿岸僧庐梵刹之首。万寿寺现为北京艺术博物馆。图 / 石艺媛

The Wanshou Temple in Haidian District, Beijing. Built in the Ming Dynasty and renovated and expanded in the Qing Dynasty, it is a large ancient architectural complex which served as a monastery, a classical garden, and a temporary imperial palace. It is the most famous Buddhist temple on the eastern bank of the Changhe River from Kunming Lake. The Wanshou Temple is now the Beijing Art Museum. Photograph by Shi Yiyuan

高梁桥，位于北京市西城区高梁河上。桥下一侧为高梁闸。现存桥为清代所建，存有旧闸槽和绞关石。图 / 王珺燕

The Gaoliang Bridge over the Gaoliang River in Xicheng District, Beijing. Under the bridge is the Gaoliang sluice. The bridge was built in the Qing Dynasty, and has old engineering structures for storage and discharge of water. Photograph by Wang Junyan

后海夜景。

永定河改道后遗留下的前海、后海、西海三个自西北向东南连续排列的弓形湖泊组成了什刹海，元代称之为积水潭，自明代起称之为什刹海。在元代，来自全国的物资商货集散于这里的码头，形成“舳舻蔽水”的景象。码头东北岸边的斜街和钟鼓楼一带是元大都城中最繁华的闹市。图 / 王旭明

Houhai at night.

The Yongding River, the largest river flowing through Beijing, was prone to change its course and cause floods. To prevent that, Qing Emperor Kangxi (1654-1722) reinforced the river's bank and fixed its course. The result was the formation of three bow-shaped lakes from northwest to southeast – Qianhai, Houhai, and Xihai. Together, they formed the Shichahai scenic area. It was called Jishuitan in the Yuan Dynasty and Shichahai since the Ming Dynasty. In the Yuan Dynasty, goods and supplies from all over the country were distributed in the wharves here, and the scene looked like "ship convoys covering the lakes". The busiest downtown areas in the Yuan capital were Xiejie Street and the Bell Tower and Drum Tower on the northeastern bank of the wharf. Photograph by Wang Xuming

前海沿岸装饰着巨型龙灯，欢庆中国农历龙年。图 / 曹静彬

The shore of Qianhai Lake is decorated with a giant dragon-shaped lantern to celebrate the Chinese Year of the Dragon. Photograph by Cao Jingbin

伫立在西海边的郭守敬雕像。图 / 赵承顺

The statue of Guo Shoujing by Xihai Lake. Photograph by Zhao Chengshun

银锭桥位于前海和后海之间，因桥形似银锭而得名。图 / 闫立军

The Yinding Bridge (Silver Ingot Bridge) connecting Qianhai and Hou-hai lakes. The bridge gets its name because it looks like a silver ingot. Photograph by Yan Lijun

万宁桥，位于什刹海东岸，是北京中轴线上最古老的桥梁，至今已有700多年历史。桥西遗存有四只镇水兽石雕，桥东存两只，其中桥东北护岸上的为元代遗存，颌下刻有“至元四年九月”，桥西设澄清上闸。图 / 王珺燕

The Wanning Bridge, located on the eastern shore of Qianhai Lake, is the oldest bridge on the Central Axis of Beijing, with a history of more than 700 years. The bridge has sculptures of four mythical beasts – the patron saints of the lake – on its western end, and two more on its eastern end. The one on the northeast bank of the bridge is a stone relic that dates back to the Yuan Dynasty, with "September of the fourth year of Yuan Emperor Huizong's reign" inscribed under its jaw. To the west of the bridge is the Upper Chengqing sluice. Photograph by Wang Junyan

东不压桥，位于北京市东城区。桥北的澄清中闸曾是漕船行至运河终点码头什刹海的必经之路。现存东西两侧闸槽。图 / 杨建国

The Dongbuya Bridge in Dongcheng District, Beijing. Once the Middle Chengqing sluice on the northern end of the bridge was the only way for ships to reach Shichahai, the terminal of the canal. The bridge still has two sluice gates on its eastern and western ends. Photograph by Yang Jianguo

玉河故道。玉河是元代通惠河在大都城的一部分，也被称为“御河”，由郭守敬于1293年主持修建，元代称为通惠河，明代以后改称玉河。2006年“北京玉河历史文化恢复工程”启动，恢复了700多年前的古玉河河道。图 / 胡利明

The old course of the Yuhe River. The engineering project of the river course was launched in 1293 in the Yuan Dynasty, under the supervision of Guo Shoujing. The Yuhe was called the Tonghui in the Yuan Dynasty and renamed Yuhe in the Ming Dynasty. In 2006, the Beijing Yuhe Historical and Cultural Restoration Project was started, and the ancient Yuhe, excavated over 700 years ago, was restored. Photograph by Hu Liming

南新仓，是明清两代储藏粮食的官仓之一，位于北京市东城区。古代修建大运河的主要目的是把物资从南方运至北方。粮仓是大运河漕运史的有力实证。图 / 戴明全

Nanxin Granary in Dongcheng District, Beijing. It was one of the official warehouses for storing grain in the Ming and Qing dynasties. The main purpose of building the Grand Canal was to transport supplies from the south to the north of China. The granary is a powerful evidence of the history of water transport on the Grand Canal. Photograph by Dai Mingquan

禄米仓，位于北京市东城区，始建于明嘉靖四十年（1561 年），是明清两朝存储京官俸米的地方。古时，朝廷官员的俸禄多以米的形式发放，称之为“禄米”。图 / 戴明全

Lumi Granary in Dongcheng District, Beijing. Built in 1561 in the Ming Dynasty, it was where the "salaries" of court officials were stored in the Ming and Qing dynasties. Back then, their salaries were mostly paid in grain, which was called *lumi*, meaning "salary grain". Photograph by Dai Mingquan

列车从北京市东便门旁的通惠河上飞驰而过。图 / 赵承顺

A train speeds past the Tonghui River near Dongbianmen in Dongcheng District, Beijing. Photograph by Zhao Chengshun

庆丰闸遗址。庆丰闸位于北京市朝阳区，始建于元至元二十九年（1292 年），现存为庆丰上闸。为保护文物，河岸的镇水兽石雕易地保存，此处水兽为仿制品。图 / 戴明全

The Qingfeng sluice in Chaoyang District, Beijing. It was built in 1292 in the Yuan Dynasty, and only the upper part remains extant today. The original stone sculptures of mythical beasts on the river bank have been preserved elsewhere in order to protect the cultural relics, and the current ones on the bank are replicas. Photograph by Dai Mingquan

平津闸遗址。平津闸位于北京市朝阳区通惠河南岸，建于元至元二十九年（1292 年），明代多次修缮。平津闸分为平津上闸、平津中闸、平津下闸。现存的平津上闸是四面环水的孤岛格局，岛上仍保留着原北岸修建的将军庙。图 / 张城

The Pingjin sluice on the southern bank of the Tonghui River in Chaoyang District, Beijing. Built in 1292 in the Yuan Dynasty, it was repaired many times in the Ming Dynasty. The sluice had an upper part, a middle part, and a lower part, but only the upper part has survived. It is now surrounded by water. However, it retains the Jiangjun Temple built on the original northern bank. Photograph by Zhang Cheng

永通桥，位于北京市通州区和朝阳区交界处，横跨通惠河，史称“陆运京储之通道”，是“明代拱卫京师四大桥”之一。永通桥是三孔联拱实心栏板石桥，中孔高度与两边次孔高度相差悬殊，这种构造是专为方便漕船通行而设计的。图 / 刘义

The Yongtong Bridge over the Tonghui River, located at the junction between Tongzhou and Chaoyang districts. It was historically known as "the passage for land transport in Beijing" and one of the "four bridges to protect the capital in the Ming Dynasty". It is a three-hole stone arch bridge with solid railings, with the middle hole much higher than the secondary ones. This structure was specially designed to facilitate the passage of ships. Photograph by Liu Yi

永通桥东的“御制朝阳门至通州石道碑”。石道碑位于北京市朝阳区，建于清雍正十一年（1733年）。碑文铭刻着朝阳门至通州修筑道路的情况，底座神兽为魑首龟趺。图 / 武辉

The Imperial Stele on the Stone-Paved Road Connecting Chaoyangmen and Tongzhou, to the east of the Yongtong Bridge. The stele, located in Chaoyang District, Beijing, was built in 1733 in the Qing Dynasty. The inscription on it provides detailed information about the construction of the road. The mythical animal on the base of the stele is the mythical dragon-headed turtle. Photograph by Wu Hui

重修朝阳门石道碑，位于北京市朝阳区，立于清代乾隆年间。图 / 武辉

The rebuilt imperial stele in Chaoyang District, Beijing. It was erected during Qing Emperor Qianlong's reign. Photograph by Wu Hui

通运桥，位于北京市通州区，始建于明万历年间。石桥南北向，三孔联拱式，两侧设有石栏，一色青砂岩，每侧各有雕狮望柱 22 根，狮子神态各异。桥北为张家湾镇城墙遗迹。镇城建于明嘉靖四十三年（1564 年）。现古城尚存南面城墙遗迹。图 / 陈燕平

The Tongyun Bridge in Tongzhou District, Beijing. It was built during Ming Emperor Shenzong's reign (1573-1620). The stone bridge is a north-to-south, three-hole stone arch bridge, with green sandstone railings on both sides and 22 carved lion pillars on each side. All the lions have different expressions. To the north of the bridge are the remains of the walls of Zhangjiawan, a town built in 1564 in the Ming Dynasty. The ruins of the southern wall of the ancient town can still be seen. Photograph by Chen Yanping

燃灯塔，始建于北周年间，历代多次重修，是北京地区建造年代最早、最高大的佛塔之一。现存古塔为辽塔形制，高56米，有13层，密檐式实心砖木结构，塔檐挂有铜铃2248枚，雕凿佛像415尊。燃灯塔是大运河漕运航标，清代诗人王维珍诗句“一枝塔影认通州”即指燃灯塔。“古塔凌云”是著名的古通州八景之首。图 / 闫立军

The Randeng Pagoda, built in the Northern Zhou Dynasty (557-581) during the Northern Dynasties, was rebuilt many times in the past. It is one of the earliest and tallest pagodas in Beijing. The extant pagoda was built in the style prevalent in the Liao Dynasty (907-1125). A solid brick-wood structure with dense eaves, it is 56 meters high and has 13 floors, but there are no windows on the upper floors. The pagoda has 2,248 bronze bells hanging on the eaves and houses 415 carved Buddha statues.

The Randeng Pagoda was a navigation beacon for water transport on the Grand Canal. Qing Dynasty poet Wang Weizhen's line "I recognize Tongzhou from the reflection of its tower" refers to the beacon burning in the Randeng Pagoda. The "sky-touching pagoda" was the first of the eight famous scenic spots of Tongzhou. Photograph by Yan Lijun

北京市通州区通惠河（图下方）与北运河（图左）的交汇处。
见证千年漕运兴衰的燃灯塔坐落其间。图 / 武辉

The intersection of the Tonghui River (below) and the North Canal (left) in Tongzhou District, Beijing. It is the location of the Randeng Pagoda that witnessed the rise and fall of canal transport for a millennium. Photograph by Wu Hui

北京市通州区温榆河、小中河、通惠河、运潮减河、北运河“五河交汇”处。历史上，北运河以潮白河为重要水源补给河道。明代，潮白河与温榆河在通州城北关附近汇聚，形成著名的通州八景之一“二水汇流”。清代道光年间，潮白河不断受到地质构造影响，弃北运河而东行，“二水汇流”逐渐演变为“五河交汇”。图 / 武辉

Five rivers intersect in Tongzhou District, Beijing: the Wenyu, Xiaozhong, Tonghui, and Yunchaojian rivers, and the North Canal. Historically, the Chaobai River was an important source for replenishing the North Canal. In the Ming Dynasty, the Chaobai and Wenyu rivers converged near the North Pass of Tongzhou, and the "two-river confluence" became one of the eight famous scenic spots of Tongzhou. During Qing Emperor Daoguang's reign (1782-1850), the Chaobai River was affected by geological formations and headed eastward, abandoning the North Canal. Then the two-river confluence gradually became a five-river confluence. Photograph by Wu Hui

2

天津
九河下梢天津卫

Tianjin
Confluence of Nine Rivers

天津是中国古代唯一有确切建城时间的城市。明永乐二年十一月二十一日（1404年12月23日），明成祖朱棣在直沽设卫，因此地水路交汇，赐名“天津”，意为天子经过的渡口。“九河下梢天津卫，三道浮桥两道关。”大致意思是指众多水系汇聚天津奔流入海。

天津市因水而生，因漕运而兴。大运河天津段北起武清区木厂闸，南至静海区九宣闸，流经静海、西青、南开、红桥、河北、北辰、武清7个区，北运河、南运河和海河最终在三岔河口汇聚，东流入海，其中，71公里长的北、南运河三岔口段列入中国大运河世界遗产河段。明清时期，大运河天津段是漕船到达京师的要道，处于京杭大运河的枢纽地位，其见证了漕船河海联运的历史和多元文化的交流。天津河海联运使妈祖文化与直沽地方文化充分结合，形成了天津妈祖文化；人们枕水而居、傍水生活，留下了西码头百忍京秧歌高跷、杨柳青木版年画等丰富的非物质文化遗产。

Tianjin is the only ancient Chinese city that has a record of the exact date when it was founded. On December 23, 1404, Ming Emperor Chengzu Zhu Di decided to set up a garrison in Zhigu, a town in today’s Tianjin. Since the area was an intersection of waterways, it was named “Tianjin”, meaning “the emperor’s ferry”. A poem goes, “Nine rivers converge in Tianjin, and there are three pontoon bridges and two passes”, a reference to the many water systems converging in Tianjin and flowing into the sea.

Tianjin was born because of water and prospered because of canal transport. The Tianjin section of the Grand Canal starts from the Muchang sluice in Wuqing District in the north, and ends at the Jiuxuan sluice in Jinghai District in the south. It flows through seven districts – Jinghai, Xiqing, Nankai, Hongqiao, Hebei, Beichen, and Wuqing. The North Canal, the South Canal, and the Haihe River converge at Sanchakou before running eastward into the sea. The 71-kilometer-long Sanchahekou stretch of the North and South Canals is listed as a World Heritage section of the Grand Canal.

During the Ming and Qing dynasties, the Tianjin section of the Grand Canal was the main route for ships to reach Beijing, the capital, making it a hub of the Beijing-Hangzhou section of the Grand Canal, and a witness to the history of river-sea transport and multicultural exchanges. Tianjin’s river-sea transport integrated the fishing community’s Mazu culture, which grew around the myth of a powerful sea goddess of the same name, with Zhigu’s local culture, forming a Tianjin Mazu culture.

The people of Tianjin lived on water in their stilt houses and by water, leaving behind rich intangible cultural heritage such as the Bairen Beijing-Style Stilt Yangko Dance at the West Pier, and the Yangliuqing New Year Woodblock Prints – originating in the town of Yangliuqing in Tianjin and used to decorate houses during the Spring Festival.

北、南运河在三岔口合流入海河，进而东流入海。北、南运河天津三岔口段河道，全长 71 公里。图 / 高爱艳

The North and South Canals merge into the Haihe River at Sanchakou, and then flow eastward into the sea. The Sanchakou section of the North and South Canals stretches over 71 kilometers. Photograph by Gao Aiyan

筐儿港水利枢纽，位于天津市武清区，历经清朝、民国和新中国三个不同时代建设，形成了集拦洪、分洪、排沥、排污和蓄水灌溉功能为一体的大型水利枢纽。图 / 张凡

The Kuang'ergang water conservancy project in Wuqing District, Tianjin. It was constructed in three historical periods – the Qing Dynasty (1616-1911), the Republic of China (1912-1949), and the People's Republic of China (1949-present) – and has today been developed into a large multipurpose water conservancy project integrating flood control, flood diversion, drainage, sewage discharge, and water storage for irrigation. Photograph by Zhang Fan

九宣闸，位于天津市静海区，始建于清光绪七年（1881年），是大运河进入天津的标志。九宣闸在纾解水患、农业灌溉、漕运交通方面都发挥了重要作用。其历经多次修缮，至今仍发挥水利功能。图 / 周炳伟

The Jiuxuan sluice in Jinghai District, Tianjin. It was built in 1881 in the Qing Dynasty, and marks the Grand Canal entering Tianjin. The sluice played an important role in alleviating floods, irrigation, and canal transport. After many repairs, it continues to play a role in local water conservancy. Photograph by Zhou Bingwei

耳闸，位于天津市河北区，始建于 1919 年，为海河分洪和通航而建。如今，呈船形的新闸与十八孔老耳闸共同组成了耳闸公园。图 / 张凡

The Er sluice in Hebei District, Tianjin. It was built in 1919 for flood diversion and navigation on the Haihe River. Today, the 18-hole old sluice and a new boat-shaped sluice are the primary attractions in the Erzha Park. Photograph by Zhang Fan

天津北、南运河交汇后合流入海河，东流入渤海。图 / 张凡

The North and South Canals converge in Tianjin, flow into the Haihe River, and then go further east into the Bohai Sea. Photograph by Zhang Fan

元明清天妃宫遗址博物馆内陈列的明代沉船。元明清天妃宫遗址博物馆位于天津河东区，是中国唯一一座妈祖文化遗址博物馆。妈祖，亦称“天妃”“天后”，俗称“海神娘娘”，是传说中掌管海上航运的女神。妈祖是闽南文化的灵魂。元代，妈祖文化随着海运北上，传到海漕终点天津，在大直沽地区兴建了天妃灵慈宫。1998 年，考古专家对天妃宫宫殿进行发掘，出土大批文物。经考古论证，大直沽为天津市城市的原生点，天妃宫则是天津城市原生点的标志。图 / 金立冬

Ming Dynasty shipwrecks in the Tianfei Palace Site Museum in Hedong District, Tianjin. The museum, displaying Yuan, Ming, and Qing memorabilia, is the only museum in China to showcase Mazu culture artifacts.

Mazu, the legendary sea goddess who presided over maritime shipping, is also known as “Tianfei”, “Tianhou”, and more commonly, the “Queen of the Ocean”. Mazu is the soul of southern Fujian culture.

In the Yuan Dynasty, Mazu culture was propagated northward by sea to Tianjin, the terminal of sea freight, and the Tianfei Palace, a temple to Mazu, was built in the Zhigu area, Tianjin.

In 1998, archaeologists excavated the Tianfei Palace and unearthed a large number of cultural relics. There is archaeological evidence that Zhigu is the birthplace of Tianjin, and the Tianfei Palace is its symbol. Photograph by Jin Lidong

大运河十四仓遗址出土的元代文物。大运河十四仓遗址位于天津武清区。元代，这里设有粮仓十四座，是元大都（今北京）外围最大的漕运仓储基地。考古专家在这里发掘出大量元至清代的文物。图 / 李胜利

Cultural relics of the Yuan Dynasty unearthed from the Shisicang site of the Grand Canal. This site, located in Wuqing District, Tianjin, was the largest grain transportation and storage base on the outskirts of Beijing, boasting 14 granaries. Here archaeologists have unearthed a large number of cultural relics from the Yuan to Qing dynasties. Photograph by Li Shengli

北洋大学堂团城旧址。北洋大学堂位于天津市红桥区北运河畔，是中国近代第一所综合性大学。团城是北洋大学保留下来的三栋建筑中历史最悠久的一栋，建于1930年前后，曾为北洋大学办公地。图 / 李胜利

The Tuancheng building in Hongqiao District, Tianjin, one of the buildings of the Peiyang University, the precursor of Tianjin University. Located on the bank of the North Canal, it was the first comprehensive university in modern China. Tuancheng is the oldest of the three preserved buildings of the university. It was constructed around 1930, and used to be the office of Peiyang University. Photograph by Li Shengli

“津西第一宅”石家大院，位于天津市西青区。这里是清末天津八大巨富之一石元仕的住宅，主体建筑始建于清光绪初年(1875年)。门前是京杭大运河流经天津的南运河。石家原籍山东，祖辈漕运发家后于清乾隆年间定居天津杨柳青镇。图 / 李胜利

Shi's Courtyard in Xiqing District, Tianjin. It was the residence of Shi Yuanshi, one of the eight richest tycoons in Tianjin in the late Qing Dynasty. The Shi family was originally from Shandong. They acquired their wealth through canal transport and then settled in Yangliuqing Town in Tianjin during Qing Emperor Qianlong's reign.

The courtyard was once known as the grandest estate in western Tianjin. The main buildings were constructed in 1875. In front of the gate is the South Canal. Photograph by Li Shengli

天后宫春祭大典。天后宫原名天妃宫，俗称“娘娘宫”，坐落于天津三岔河口之海河西岸。农历腊月廿三，元、明、清历代王朝均派使臣代表皇帝来此祭祀，形成天后宫传统的皇家高规格春祭活动。天津天后宫春祭大典于 2007 年恢复举办。图 / 崔宪伟

The Spring Festival ceremony at the Tianfei Palace. The Tianfei Palace, a restored temple of sea goddess Mazu, lies on the west bank of the Haihe River at Sanchahekou.

During the Yuan, Ming and Qing dynasties, on the 23rd day of the 12th Chinese lunar month, the emperor would send his envoys to worship here on his behalf. In this way it became a royal tradition to hold a magnificent Spring Festival ceremony at the Tianfei Palace. The tradition was resumed in 2007. Photograph by Cui Xianwei

妈祖祭典（天津皇会）期间举行的非遗展演巡游。农历三月廿三日是妈祖诞辰，在这一天，以天后宫为中心会举办大型民间酬神庙会活动，经过几百年积淀，逐渐形成集神祇崇拜、祈愿还福、赛会表演等于一体的庙会，俗称妈祖祭典、天津皇会。这同时也成就了天津最著名的商业街——宫南宫北大街（今古文化街）。妈祖祭典是大运河天津段重要非物质文化遗产，已被列入国家级非物质文化遗产代表性项目名录。图 / 金立冬

An intangible cultural heritage parade during the Mazu Festival. Sea goddess Mazu's birthday is celebrated on the 23rd day of the third Chinese lunar month, when a large folk temple fair is held around the Tianfei Palace. Held for centuries, this temple fair, commonly known as the Mazu Festival, or the Tianjin Imperial Fair, is an amalgamation of praying for blessings and folk performances.

Thanks to the fair, the street running south to north of the temple, now known as the Ancient Culture Street, has become the most famous commercial street in Tianjin.

The Mazu Festival is an important intangible cultural heritage in the Tianjin section of the Grand Canal, and has been included in the list of national intangible cultural heritage representative projects. Photograph by Jin Lidong

天津古文化街戏楼前举行非遗展演。图 / 马春林

An intangible cultural heritage performance in front of the theater on the Ancient Culture Street in Tianjin. Photograph by Ma Chunlin

农历大年初一，人们在天津古文化街选购杨柳青年画。杨柳青木版年画始于明，盛于清，传承数百年，号称中国四大年画之首，2006 年被列入首批国家级非物质文化遗产名录。

千年古镇杨柳青被京杭大运河穿镇而过。这里是杨柳青木版年画的发源地，孕育了中国的“赶大营”文化；包括风筝、剪纸、砖雕、石刻、彩塑、花会在内的民间传统艺术在这里绵延流传。杨柳青古镇被誉为“北国江南”“沽上扬州”。图 / 佟郁

People buy Yangliuqing New Year Woodblock Prints on the Ancient Culture Street in Tianjin, on the first day of the Chinese Lunar New Year.

The woodblock prints originated in the Ming Dynasty, flourished in the Qing Dynasty, and have been passed down for centuries. It is known as one of the four major New Year prints in China, and was listed among the first group of national intangible cultural heritage arts in 2006.

The Beijing-Hangzhou Grand Canal runs through Yangliuqing in Tianjin. This 1,000-year-old town is the birthplace of the Yangliuqing New Year Woodblock Prints. Besides the prints, traditional folk arts including kites, paper-cutting, brick carving, stone carving, colored sculptures, and folk performances spread from here, handed down generation after generation. The ancient town is also called “the southern water town of the north” and “the Yangzhou on Zhigu”. Photograph by Tong Yu

春节期间，杨柳青年画舞蹈队在运河边表演舞蹈《百子闹春》。舞蹈队将年画与舞蹈巧妙结合，从杨柳青年画《连年有余》《五子夺莲》《放风筝》《戏蝈蝈》中取材，创编了大型年画组舞《百子闹春》。每逢春节及重大活动，舞蹈队就献上精彩表演。图 / 崔宪伟

The Yangliuqing Dance Troupe performs a New Year dance, *A Hundred Sons Greet Spring*, by the Grand Ganal. The dancers skillfully displayed the traditional New Year images with their dance, drawing inspiration from the local woodblock prints such as *Harvests Year after Year*, *Flying Kites*, and *Playing with Grasshoppers*. The troupe puts up a wonderful performance every Spring Festival and on other major occasions. Photograph by Cui Xianwei

杨柳青大运河国家文化公园上演“小车汇”秧歌。图 / 金立冬

The Xiaochehui Yangko Dance, a kind of folk dance with floats as the main props, staged in the Yangliuqing Grand Canal Park. Photograph by Jin Lidong

西码头百忍京秧歌高跷表演。这是天津民俗文化典型代表之一。“西码头”是天津地区的老地名，位于现红桥区南运河南岸，昔日这里漕运发达，聚居着靠码头搬运糊口的人群。西码头百忍京秧歌创会于清嘉庆二十四年（1819年），北京人蔡少文到天津西码头传授北京的高跷秧歌，授予北京南城的练法、西城的唱调、“老三点”的鼓点，在西码头形成了独家独派的高跷秧歌表演方式。图 / 马桂兰

The Bairen Beijing-Style Stilt Yangko Dance at the West Pier. It is a typical form of Tianjin folk culture.

The West Pier is located on the southern bank of the South Canal in Hongqiao District, Tianjin. In the past, this used to be a prosperous area because of the flourishing canal transport.

The West Pier Bairen Beijing-Style Yangko Society was founded in 1819 in the Qing Dynasty. Cai Shaowen, a Beijing native, went to the West Pier to teach the locals Beijing's Stilt Yangko, a combination of stilt walking and the Yangko, a farmers' dance to pray for a good harvest. In this way the dance form of southern Beijing, the singing style of western Tianjin, and the traditional drum were fused to form a Stilt Yangko performance unique to the West Pier. Photograph by Ma Guilan

魅力元宝岛

津沽福地

河北
一船明月过沧州

3

Hebei
The Boat Passes Cangzhou Under a Bright Moon

"长河日暮乱烟浮，红叶萧萧两岸秋。夜半不知行远近，一船明月过沧州。"红叶带来浓浓秋意，曲长的河道上暮烟浮动，清代诗人孙谔乘船沿着运河，夜过沧州；水上行舟的意境穿越历史长河定格在沧州上空的明月和至今仍流淌吟唱的运河上。千百年来，大运河不但成就了沧州这个运河之城，也润泽了锦绣河北、燕赵大地。

大运河河北段，始于东汉末年，历经多个朝代疏浚整治和自然改道，由北运河、南运河、卫运河、卫河及永济渠遗址组成，流经廊坊、沧州、衡水、邢台、邯郸5个市的17个县（市、区）。

大运河河北段至今仍保存着完整的古代漕运河道、堤防，三弯抵一闸、糯米大坝、捷地分洪等水利设施，展示出古代人的智慧。沧州武术、吴桥杂技、青县哈哈腔等民间传统文化艺术在运河边诞生、演化，泊头清真寺、马厂炮台等文化遗产反映出昔日的兴盛。

"Smoke covers the long river at dusk. And on both its banks red leaves rustle. In the middle of the night, I don't know how far I have traveled, and the boat passes Cangzhou under a bright moon." Qing Dynasty poet Sun E traveled by boat along the Grand Canal and passed the city of Cangzhou at night. For thousands of years, the Grand Canal has not only given Cangzhou an identity as a canal city but also made Hebei fertile.

The Hebei section of the Grand Canal, which was constructed in the late Eastern Han Dynasty (25-220), underwent dredging and natural diversion during subsequent dynasties. Today, it consists of the North and South Canals, the Wei Canal, the Weihe River, and the site of Yongji Canal, and flows through five cities – Langfang, Cangzhou, Hengshui, Xingtai, and Handan.

The Hebei section of the Grand Canal still preserves the ancient channel and embankments, as well as water conservancy facilities such as "three bends functioning as one sluice", the "Glutinous Rice Embankment" (Xiejia Embankment), and the Jiedi flood diversion sluice, showing the wisdom of the ancient Chinese. Traditional folk culture and arts such as Cangzhou martial arts, Wuqiao acrobatics, and the local Hahaqiang Opera were born and evolved along the canal. Its cultural heritage such as the Botou Mosque and Machang Fort reflects the prosperity of the past.

南运河沧州市区段。

沧州是大运河流经里程最长的城市，大运河沧州段长达 216 公里。

南运河的海拔落差大，水流急。元明清历代整修南运河时，设计了众多弯道，减弱水流对堤岸的冲击，保障通航顺畅。这种弯道设计，被称作“三弯抵一闸”。图 / 陈秀峰

The Cangzhou section of the South Canal, Cangzhou City, Hebei.

The Grand Canal flows through Cangzhou for the longest stretch. The Cangzhou section is 216 kilometers long.

The South Canal has a large altitude difference and a rapid current. When it was renovated in the Yuan, Ming and Qing dynasties, bends were designed to reduce the impact of the water on the embankments and ensure smooth navigation. This kind of bend design is called "three bends functioning as one sluice". Photograph by Chen Xiufeng

南运河在沧州市区的一段河道呈现出“Ω”形大弯。通过环境治理与生态修复，这里已成为运河公园。图 / 孙博育

A section of the South Canal in downtown Cangzhou, Hebei has a large omega-shaped bend. Environmental governance and ecological restoration have transformed it into a canal park. Photograph by Sun Boyu

南川老街，位于沧州市运河区，背靠南川古渡。老街南川楼、朗吟楼两座复建古迹，见证了沧州盐业和漕运的发展，现已成为运河文化新地标。图 / 李建民

Nanchuan Old Street in the Yunhe District of Cangzhou City, Hebei. It leads to the ancient Nanchuan Ferry. Two restored historical sites on the street, Nanchuan Tower and Langyin Tower, have witnessed the development of the salt industry and canal transport in Cangzhou, and have now become new landmarks of canal culture. Photograph by Li Jianmin

谢家坝，位于沧州市，于清朝末年由谢姓乡绅捐资修建。

大坝全长 218 米，厚 3.6 米，高 5 米，由糯米熬粥加灰土与泥土混合筑成，也被称为“糯米大坝”。图 / 陈秀峰

The Xiejia Embankment in Cangzhou City, Hebei. It was built in the late Qing Dynasty with donations from a member of the local gentry, surnamed Xie.

The embankment is 218 meters long, 3.6 meters thick, and 5 meters high. It was built with glutinous rice, lime, and soil, hence known as the “Glutinous Rice Embankment”. Photograph by Chen Xiufeng

古老的捷地分洪闸（图右下方）与年轻的捷地新建闸分别横跨于捷地减河与南运河主河道上。

The old Jiedi flood diversion sluice (bottom right) and the new Jiedi sluice straddle the Jiedijian River and the main channel of the South Canal respectively.

捷地减河及分洪闸，位于沧县捷地镇。捷地减河是南运河的主要分洪河道，开挖于明朝弘治三年（1490年）。清朝乾隆三十六年（1771年），分洪闸闸门改为龙骨石坝，便于骤溢河水流入减河。图 / 周炳伟

The Jiedi distributary and flood diversion sluice in Jiedi Town, Cangxian County, Hebei. The Jiedi distributary is the main flood diversion channel of the South Canal, excavated in 1490 in the Ming Dynasty. In 1771 in the Qing Dynasty, the sluice was replaced by a stone dam to facilitate sudden overflows of river water into the distributary. Photograph by Zhou Bingwei

民国时期，捷地分洪闸设施安装上了德国造的分洪设备。图 / 邢雨龙

During the Republic of China period, flood diversion equipment made in Germany was installed at the Jiedi flood diversion sluice. Photograph by Xing Yulong

沧县捷地乡御碑苑内的“御诗碑”，铭刻着清代乾隆皇帝的两首题诗，是乾隆亲自主抓水利工程的“手记”。图 / 张海军

The Imperial Poetry Stele in the Imperial Stele Garden in Jiedi Township, Cangxian County, Hebei. The stele bears two poems written by Qing Emperor Qianlong. They were the emperor's "notes" when he took personal charge of water conservancy projects. Photograph by Zhang Haijun

沧县捷地乡御碑苑内的“宪示碑”，立于清同治年间，碑文大意为“无论官兵还是百姓，都不得在两条河的堤岸上取土，不得在河坝上下钉橛、置网、捕鱼”。图 / 邢雨龙

The Statute Stele in the Imperial Stele Garden. It was erected during Qing Emperor Tongzhi's reign (1862-1875). The inscription on the stele says, "Both military staff and civilians are prohibited from taking soil from the banks of the two rivers, nailing pegs on the embankments, setting up nets, and fishing." Photograph by Xing Yulong

沧州市博物馆馆藏的国家一级文物——三彩刻宝相花纹盘。俗话说，“三彩挂蓝，价值连连”，这是因为唐三彩中的蓝色釉料含钴矿物依赖进口，较为稀少。图 / 邢雨龙

A national first-class cultural relic in Cangzhou Museum: a tri-colored plate engraved with a composite floral design. There is a saying that “when tri-colored glaze includes blue color, it is worth more.” That is because the blue glaze in the tri-colored glazed pottery of the Tang Dynasty contains cobalt, which was rare and mainly imported. Photograph by Xing Yulong

泊头清真寺古建筑群，坐落于泊头市古运河西岸，始建于明永乐二年（1404 年）。以水为胜，以河生地，以航达裕，民有其富，城有其罄，是为泊头。泊头因运河漕运兴起而得名。泊头清真寺历经多次重修扩建，融回汉风格于一体，被称为“华北清真第一寺”。该建筑群主要建筑都在中轴线上，这也是中国古代建筑的典型特征。图 / 张海军

The ancient Botou Mosque architecture complex stands on the west bank of the Grand Canal in Botou City, Hebei. It was built in 1404 in the Ming Dynasty. Botou, meaning “the wharf where boats are moored”, prospered due to canal transport. The Botou Mosque, which has been renovated and expanded many times, combines the Hui and Han ethnic styles. It is known as the “No. 1 mosque in north China”. The main buildings are located on the central axis, which is a typical feature of ancient Chinese architecture. Photograph by Zhang Haijun

马厂炮台遗址，大运河沧州段唯一的军事设施遗迹。炮台建于清同治十年（1871 年），现存中央炮台一座及东西营区十多座炮台。

保存较好的中央炮台占地约 1.1 万平方米，炮台上修有炮位、暗道、排水道等。图 / 王相智

The ruins of the Machang Fort are the only military ruins along the Cangzhou section of the Grand Canal. The fort, built in 1871 in the Qing Dynasty, has a central barbette and more than 10 barbettes in its east and west camps.

The well-preserved central barbette, with an area of about 11,000 square meters, has gun emplacements, secret passages, and drainage channels. Photograph by Wang Xiangzhi

呈 S 形弯的大运河河道，位于故城县郑口镇。这段河道水流湍急，多次漫堤决口，明朝时期就开始治理，民国二十三年（1934 年）开始修建挑水坝。挑水坝是一种护岸丁坝，其轴线与水流斜交，挑开大溜，保护下游堤段。郑口挑水坝现存 6 处，呈倒 U 形分布在河堤内侧。图 / 牟明宏

大运河故城县段郑口挑水坝（1986 年摄）。
图 / 韩振明

The Grand Canal's spur dikes in Zhengkou Township, Gucheng County, Hebei. This photo was taken in 1986. Photograph by Han Zhenming

The Grand Canal has an S-shaped section in Zhengkou Township, Gucheng County, Hebei. The river was turbulent in this section and often overflowed its embankments. The problem was addressed during the Ming Dynasty. Subsequently, in 1934, spur dikes were constructed to divert the flow and protect downstream embankments. There are six spur dikes in Zhengkou. Photograph by Mu Minghong

华家口夯土险工“糯米大坝”，位于衡水景县华家口村，修建于清朝末年，全长 255 米，呈梯形，南北走向。图 / 张帆

The “Glutinous Rice Embankment” at Huajiakou Village, Jingxian County, Hebei. Built in the late Qing Dynasty, it is 255 meters long and shaped like a trapezoid, running north to south. Photograph by Zhang Fan

油坊码头及险工遗址，位于邢台市清河县，建于明清，因油坊商贾云集而得名。图 / 邢东魁

The Youfang Wharf and revetment in Qinghe County, Xingtai City, Hebei. Built in the Ming and Qing dynasties, it was named after a concentration of oil mills here. Photograph by Xing Dongkui

大名府故城城墙遗址，位于邯郸市。

大运河大名段历史悠久，肇始于三国时期，兴盛于隋唐，渐衰于明清，直至 20 世纪 70 年代末，河道水量大减，近乎荒废。运河沿岸历史文化遗存众多，包括大名府故城遗址、大名天主教堂等。图 / 宋现彬

The ruins of the ancient city walls of Daming in Handan City, Hebei.

The Daming section of the Grand Canal has a long history. It began in the Three Kingdoms period, flourished in the Sui and Tang dynasties, and gradually declined in the Ming and Qing dynasties. In the 1970s, the volume of the river was reduced, and the channel was almost abandoned. There are many historical and cultural sites along this section, including the ruins of the ancient town of Daming and the Daming Catholic Church. Photograph by Song Xianbin

大名天主教堂。图 / 宋现彬

The Daming Catholic Church, Handan City, Hebei.
Photograph by Song Xianbin

邺城三台遗址前矗立着一座曹操雕像。邯郸市临漳县古称邺城，始建于春秋，曾为六朝古都（曹魏、后赵、冉魏、前燕、东魏、北齐）。邺城三台遗址得名于曹操定都邺城后修筑的用于军事防御、举办庆典和活动的三座高大台榭（由南向北依次是金凤台、铜雀台、冰井台）。大运河邯郸段肇始于东汉末期，形成于隋，繁荣于唐宋。临漳县运河故道被淤埋在现地表下，地上已无痕迹。图 / 宋现彬

A statue of Cao Cao (155-220), the founder of the Wei Kingdom in the Three Kingdoms period, at the Santai site in the ancient town of Yecheng, Hebei. Yecheng, now Linzhang County in Handan City, was founded in the Spring and Autumn Period and was the ancient capital of six dynasties.

The Santai site is the remnant of three tall pavilions (Jinfeng, Tongque, and Bingjing) built for military defense, celebrations, and events after Cao Cao made Yecheng the capital of Wei.

The Handan section of the Grand Canal was built in the late Eastern Han Dynasty, was developed in the Sui Dynasty, and flourished in the Tang and Song (960-1279) dynasties. The old river course in Linzhang County was silted and lies buried, leaving no trace aboveground. Photograph by Song Xianbin

沧州武术表演。沧州是中国武术发源地之一。由于地理、历史条件关系，沧州武术素有“武建泱泱乎有表海雄风”之说。图 / 金洁

A Cangzhou martial arts performance. Cangzhou is one of the birthplaces of Chinese martial arts. Geographical and historical conditions have made Cangzhou martial arts magnificent and unparalleled. Photograph by Jin Jie

哈哈腔演出。哈哈腔是河北民间地方剧种，约形成于明末清初，由民间弦索小曲演变而来，讲述人民在生活和劳动中所经历的故事。图 / 王占林

A Hahaqiang Opera performance. This folk opera of Hebei evolved from Chinese folk string instrument music and developed in the late Ming and early Qing dynasties. The opera tells stories of local people's work and life. Photograph by Wang Zhanlin

杂技演员在吴桥码头练习杂技。

大运河边的吴桥县是中国杂技发源地之一，是著名的“杂技之乡”。吴桥杂技最早可追溯至汉代。大运河贯通后，沿河流域码头、城镇兴起，吴桥杂技艺人乘船沿大运河北上南下表演，清末已开始走出国门，走进东南亚，甚至远渡重洋巡游欧美。图 / 陈秀峰

Acrobats practice at the Wuqiao Wharf, Wuqiao County, Hebei.

Wuqiao along the Grand Canal is one of the cradles of Chinese acrobatics. Wuqiao acrobatics can be traced back to the Han Dynasty (206 BC-AD 220). After the Grand Canal was opened, wharves and towns sprang up along the canal basin. Then Wuqiao acrobats began taking boats along the canal to perform further north and south. In the late Qing Dynasty, they went to Southeast Asia, and even traveled across the ocean to Europe and America. Photograph by Chen Xiufeng

4

山东
江上帆樯万斛来

Shandong
A River Crowned with Thousands of Masts

“官船贾舶纷纷过，击鼓鸣锣处处闻。”“城中烟火千家集，江上帆樯万斛来。”明代大学者李东阳（1447—1516）在《过鳌头矶》中描绘了山东聊城市临清钞关附近运河沿岸的景象——漕运鼎盛，帆樯如林，锣鼓喧鸣，运河人家。大运河给昔日的齐鲁大地带来了一水繁华。

大运河山东段位于大运河中枢区段，流经德州、聊城、泰安、济宁和枣庄5个市，沿线地区与苏皖豫冀四省交界，在历史上曾经是沟通北方政治中心和南方经济中心的“生命线”，是南粮北运、商旅交通、军资调配的交通动脉，有“国家漕运江南四百万，寄径于山东漕河一线”之称。

大运河山东段有8段河道、15个遗产点列入中国大运河世界遗产点段，包括南运河德州段、会通河临清段（元运河、明运河）、会通河阳谷段、会通河南旺枢纽段、小汶河、会通河微山段、中河台儿庄段以及临清运河钞关、汶上南旺分水枢纽、东平戴村坝等诸多河道、水利工程设施遗存。沿线的非物质文化遗产如端鼓腔、梁山武术、鲁南皮影、鲁南花鼓等，根植于齐鲁文化，融合吸纳南北文化，释放出诚信、仁义、包容、开放、多元的鲁风运河文化特质。

“Official ships and merchant ships pass by, and drums and gongs are heard everywhere.” “The town is lit up by the lamps of hundreds of households, and the river is crowned with thousands of masts.” In his poem *Passing Aotouji*, Ming Dynasty scholar Li Dongyang (1447-1516) describes the bustling scene in the Linqing canal transport taxation office in Liaocheng, Shandong – prosperous canal transport, a forest of sails, the clamor of gongs and drums, and the multitude of people living by canal. The Grand Canal brought prosperity to Shandong, the land of the Qi and Lu kingdoms in the past.

The Shandong section is the central section of the Grand Canal. Here, the Grand Canal flows through five cities – Dezhou, Liaocheng, Tai’an, Jining, and Zaozhuang. Historically, this section was the “lifeline” of China, connecting the northern political center and the southern economic center. It was the traffic artery for grain shipment, commercial travel, and transfer of military supplies from the south to the north. A popular saying goes, “Grain produced south of the Yangtze is shipped to the north annually, all thanks to the Shandong section of the Grand Canal.”

The Shandong section has eight river stretches and 15 heritage sites listed as World Heritage Site of the Grand Canal. The river sections are: the Dezhou section of the South Canal, the Linqing section of the Huitong River (the Yuan Canal and the Ming Canal), the Yanggu section of the Huitong River, the Nanwang section of the Huitong River, the Weishan Section of the Xiaowenhe River, the Weishan section of the Huitong River, and the Tai’erzhuang section of the Zhonghe River. The heritage sites include the remnants of facilities, such as the Linqing canal transport taxation office, the Nanwang streamflow division hub in Wenshang County, and the Daicun Dam in Dongping County.

There is also an abundance of intangible cultural heritage along the route, such as the Duangu Opera, Liangshan martial arts, the southern Shandong shadow play, and the southern Shandong Flower Drum Opera. These folk arts are rooted in the Qi-Lu culture of the past kingdoms of Qi and Lu. The cultural fusion between the north and the south gave rise to the Shandong canal culture, which is characterized by integrity, benevolence, inclusiveness, openness, and diversity.

德州市德城区丰乐屯村拍摄的南运河。南运河德州段全长 45 公里，至今保留着“九龙十八弯”的原生古河道形态。图 / 刘克政

The South Canal in Fengletun Village, Dezhou City, Shandong.

The Dezhou section of the South Canal, 45 kilometers long, retains the original river course with its "18 bends resembling nine dragons". Photograph by Liu Kezheng

四女寺枢纽，位于德州市德城区、武城县和河北故城县三县（区）交界处，上游接卫运河，下游分别接减河、岔河和南运河，是目前海河平原规模最大的水闸工程建筑群，既能分洪除涝，又能灌溉、输水、航运。图 / 刘克政

The Sinüsi water conservancy hub, located at the junction of Shandong's Decheng District and Wucheng County of Dezhou City, and Hebei's Gucheng County.

The hub is connected to the Wei Canal upstream, and the Jianhe River, the Chahe River and the South Canal downstream. It is the largest sluice complex on the Haihe Plain, with multiple functions such as flood diversion, irrigation, and shipment. Photograph by Liu Kezheng

苏禄王墓，坐落于德州大运河畔。

古苏禄国位于菲律宾南部，明朝时期，苏禄国三位国王东王、西王和峒王带领使团访问中国。他们沿京杭大运河北行，最终到达北京。返程行至德州时，苏禄东王突发急症去世，明朝廷以王礼为其安葬，并修建了这座宏伟的陵墓。图 / 刘克政

The tomb of the King of Sulu on the bank of the Grand Canal in Dezhou City, Shandong.

The Sulu Kingdom was an ancient kingdom in the southern Philippines. In the Ming Dynasty, three kings of Sulu, the East King, the West King, and the Tong King, came to the court with their entourage. They traveled north along the Beijing-Hangzhou Grand Canal and finally arrived in Beijing. On the return trip, the East King died of an illness in Dezhou. The Ming emperor ordered a royal burial for him, and a magnificent mausoleum was built in his honor. Photograph by Liu Kezheng

在运河名城、千年古县临清，元运河和明运河纵贯城区呈巨大“人”字，然后分别和卫运河（永济渠）相融。图片中下方河道为明运河，右为元运河，上方为卫运河。图 / 何新华

In Linqing, a famous county with a millennium-old history, the Yuan Canal and the Ming Canal run through the downtown area in the shape of a herringbone, and then merge with the Wei Canal (the Yongji Canal). The photograph shows the Wei Canal at the top, the Yuan Canal to the right, and the Ming Canal at the bottom. Photograph by He Xinhua

会通桥，原为会通闸，始建于元代，明永乐年间改建为桥。

临清城区元运河河道上有三座古桥——问津桥、会通桥、月径桥，俗称“玉带三桥”。图 / 何新华

The Huitong Bridge in Liaocheng City, Shandong.

It was formerly the Huitong sluice built in the Yuan Dynasty, and was converted into a bridge during Ming Emperor Yongle's reign (1403-1424).

There are three ancient bridges over the Yuan Canal in Linqing, Liaocheng: Wenjin, Huitong, and Yuejing, collectively known as "The Three Jade Belt Bridges". Photograph by He Xinhua

问津桥，原为临清闸，始建于元代，明万历年间改建为桥。图 / 何新华

The Wenjin Bridge in Liaocheng City, Shandong.

It was formerly the Linqing sluice built in the Yuan Dynasty, and was converted into a bridge during Ming Emperor Wanli's reign (1573-1620). Photograph by He Xinhua

月径桥，位于问津桥与会通桥之间，清顺治年间由徽商邵以枢捐资修建。图 / 何新华

The Yuejing Bridge in Liaocheng City, Shandong.

Standing between the Wenjin Bridge and the Huitong Bridge, it was built with donations from Shao Yishu, a Huizhou merchant, during Qing Emperor Shunzhi's reign (1644-1661). Photograph by He Xinhua

鳌头矶，位于临清市元运河与明运河的接合处，是一组结构精巧、古朴典雅的楼阁式建筑。鳌是古代传说中海里的大龟或大鳖。此楼阁得名于此地一座形如鳌头的石坝，运河上的四处河闸像鳌的两对足，广济桥似其尾。图 / 何新华

Aotouji in Linqing County, Liaocheng City, Shandong.

Located at the junction of the Yuan Canal and the Ming Canal, it has a cluster of elegant pavilion-style buildings with exquisite structure. *Ao* is a giant sea turtle in ancient Chinese myth. The complex got its name from a stone dam shaped like the head of an *Ao*, with the four sluices on the canal imagined to be its four feet, and the Guangji Bridge its tail. Photograph by He Xinhua

临清运河钞关，始建于明宣德四年（1429 年），是明清两代中央政府设于运河上督理漕运税收的直属机构，为古代八大钞关之一。图 / 隋青

The Linqing canal transport taxation office in Liaocheng City, Shandong.

Established in 1429 during Ming Emperor Xuande's reign, it was directly administered by the central government in the Ming and Qing dynasties. The Lingqin office was one of the eight canal transport taxation offices. Photograph by Sui Qing

临清砖闸，位于临清明运河上。在明清两代，临清砖闸与明运河入卫南板闸（头闸）上下互联、前后起闭，构成漕运管控体系，确保漕运顺利进行。图 / 司建平

The Linqing brick pass on the Ming Canal in Linqing County, Liaocheng City, Shandong.

In the Ming and Qing dynasties, the Linqing brick pass and the southern sluice (the head sluice) connecting the Ming Canal and the Wei Canal were interconnected to form a circular control system to ensure the smooth operation of canal transport. Photograph by Si Jianping

临清舍利宝塔，坐落在城北郊，建于明万历年间，塔高60余米，是山东省仅存的一座明塔。图 / 司建平

The Budda Relics Pagoda in Linqing County, Liaocheng City, Shandong.

Located in the northern suburbs of Linqing, the pagoda was built during Ming Emperor Wanli's reign (1573-1620). Over 60 meters high, it is the only surviving Ming pagoda in Shandong. Photograph by Si Jianping

临清戴湾闸。闸畔原建有“闸官衙门”和“主簿厅”，共同管理闸务和漕政。图 / 司建平

The Daiwan sluice in Linqing County, Liaocheng City, Shandong.

Originally, there was a Sluice Office and a Canal Transport Secretariat beside the sluice. Photograph by Si Jianping

聊城山陕会馆，坐落于东关古运河西岸，由清代山西、陕西商人集资合建，包含 160 多间亭台楼阁。图 / 司建平

The Shanxi-Shaanxi Guild Hall in Liaocheng City, Shandong.

It is located on the west bank of the Dongguan ancient canal. Built by merchants from Shanxi and Shaanxi in the Qing Dynasty, it has more than 160 pavilions and towers. Photograph by Si Jianping

聊城古城被东昌湖环绕，如漂浮在水面上的岛，“千里运河第一楼”——光岳楼屹立在岛中央。聊城以中国“江北水城 · 运河古都”著称。大运河从聊城境内西侧穿过，为聊城带来了数百年的经济和文化繁荣。图 / 祖军

The ancient city of Liaocheng, surrounded by Dongchang Lake, looks like an island floating on water. The Guangyue Pavilion, hailed as “the No.1 pavilion along the Grand Canal”, stands in the center of the ancient city.

Liaocheng is known as “an water town north of the Yangtze” and “an ancient capital along the Grand Canal”. The canal passes through the west part of Liaocheng, bringing the city economic and cultural prosperity for centuries. Photograph by Zu Jun

会通河阳谷县张秋段生态环境良好。图 / 李炜

The Zhangqiu section of the Huitong River in Yanggu County, Liaocheng City, Shandong. It has an excellent eco-environment. Photograph by Li Wei

阿城上闸，位于聊城市阳谷县。闸体用青石砌成，雁翅上有镇水石兽。

中国大运河会通河阳谷段修建有阿城上下闸、荆门上下闸。图 / 段更阳

The Acheng upper sluice in Yanggu County, Liaocheng City, Shandong.

The sluice is built of limestone, and on its extension there are stone-carved mythical beasts, believed to have the power to tame the flood. The Acheng upper and lower sluices and the Jingmen upper and lower sluices are located in the Yanggu section of the Huitong River. Photograph by Duan Gengyang

阿城下闸。图 / 段更阳

The closed Acheng lower sluice in Yanggu County, Liaocheng City, Shandong. Photograph by Duan Gengyang

荆门上闸所在河道的河边有石刻镇水兽，头上的文字因年代久远已模糊不清。图 / 段更阳

A stone-carved flood-taming beast stands on the bank of the Jingmen upper sluice in Yanggu County, Liaocheng City, Shandong. The sculpture has an inscription on its head which has become blurred due to its age. Photograph by Duan Gengyang

荆门下闸东侧闸墩现存一尊高约 1.2 米的石狮。图 / 段更阳

A stone lion about 1.2 meters high stands on the pier on the east side of the Jingmen lower sluice in Yanggu County, Liaocheng City, Shandong. Photograph by Duan Gengyang

南旺水利枢纽中的戴村坝，位于泰安市东平县，建于明朝。

戴村坝全长1599.5米，是保障明清两代近600年大运河最高段的会通河水源供给、实现漕运畅通的关键，被誉为“中国古代第一坝”“运河之心”。图 / 段更阳

The Daicun Dam, a part of the Nanwang water diversion hub, in Dongping County, Tai'an City, Shandong.

Built in the Ming Dynasty, the nearly 1,600-meter-long dam is critical for smooth canal transport and adequate water supply for the Huitong River – the highest section of the Grand Canal in the Ming and Qing dynasties for nearly 600 years. The Daicun Dam is known as the “No.1 dam in ancient China” and “the heart of the Grand Canal”. Photograph by Duan Gengyang

南旺分水龙王庙，位于济宁市汶上县南旺镇汶水入运的分水处，毗连南旺分水枢纽工程。大运河南旺分水枢纽工程，建于明朝，代表了17 世纪工业革命前世界土木工程和水工技术的最高成就。图 / 段更阳

The Dragon King Water Diversion Temple in Nanwang Town, Jining City, Shandong.

It is adjacent to the Nanwang water diversion hub built in the Ming Dynasty. The Nanwang hub is regarded as the most advanced civil engineering and water conservancy feat in the 17th century prior to the Industrial Revolution. Photograph by Duan Gengyang

分水龙王庙建筑群。图 / 段更阳

The Dragon King Water Diversion Temple complex in Nanwang Town, Jining City, Shandong. Photograph by Duan Gengyang

南旺分水枢纽常鸣斗门（进水口门）遗址。图 / 段更阳

The ruins of the Changming water inlet gate of the Nanwang water diversion hub in Jining City, Shandong. Photograph by Duan Gengyang

南旺分水枢纽码头砖石堤岸的明弘治十年官砖。图 / 段更阳

The wharf of the Nanwang water diversion hub in Jining City, Shandong. It was built with bricks manufactured in 1497 during Ming Emperor Hongzhi's reign. Photograph by Duan Gengyang

汶上县小汶河河道。图 / 段更阳

The Xiaowenhe River in Wenshang County, Jining City, Shandong. Photograph by Duan Gengyang

邢通斗门，位于汶上县南旺镇，建于明朝，是大运河与南旺湖的连接斗门。图 / 段更阳

The Xingtong water inlet gate in Nanwang Town, Jining City, Shandong.

Built in the Ming Dynasty, it connects the Grand Canal and Nanwang Lake. Photograph by Duan Gengyang

徐建口斗门，位于汶上县南旺镇，建于明朝，是沟通连接小汶河与马踏湖的重要减水闸。图 / 段更阳

The Xujiankou water inlet gate in Nanwang Town, Jining City, Shandong.

Built in the Ming Dynasty, it was an important distributary sluice connecting the Xiaowenhe River and the Mata Lake. Photograph by Duan Gengyang

十里闸，位于汶上县南旺镇。图 / 段更阳

The Shili sluice in Nanwang Town, Jining City, Shandong. Photograph by Duan Gengyang

柳林闸，位于汶上县南旺镇，常与十里闸协同开闭。图 / 段更阳

The Liulin sluice in Nanwang Town, Jining City, Shandong.

It was often opened and closed in coordination with the Shili sluice. Photograph by Duan Gengyang

寺前铺闸，位于汶上县南旺镇，是配合十里闸与柳林闸进行水量控制的辅助闸门。图 / 段更阳

The Siqianpu sluice in Nanwang Town, Jining City, Shandong.

It was an auxiliary sluice for streamflow control in coordination with the Shili and Liulin sluices. Photograph by Duan Gengyang

会通河微山段，位于济宁市微山湖中，长约 9.2 公里，
是大运河全段唯一一段湖中运道。图 / 秦凤森

The Weishan section of the Huitong River, located in Weishan Lake in Jining City, Shandong.

This section, over nine kilometers long, is the only part of the Grand Canal that lies in a lake. Photograph by Qin Fengsen

利建闸，位于济宁市微山县，是明清南阳新河建成的 9 座节制闸之一。图 / 陈保成

The Lijian sluice in Weishan County, Jining City, Shandong.

It was one of the nine sluices built on the Nanyang Xinhe Canal in the Ming and Qing dynasties. Photograph by Chen Baocheng

金口坝，位于济宁市兖州区，长约123米，集交通、灌溉、济运、防洪、蓄水、游览等功能于一体。图 / 王钰

The Jinkou Dam in Yanzhou District, Jining City, Shandong.

The nearly 123-meter-long dam has multipronged functions such as canal transport, irrigation, flood control, water storage, and sightseeing. Photograph by Wang Yu

台儿庄古城，位于枣庄市，处于京杭大运河中心点，城内拥有 3 公里古运河河道和 15 公里水街水巷，被誉为“运河文化的活化石”。京杭大运河枣庄段至今仍是南北航运的重要枢纽。图 / 张卫国

The ancient town of Tai'erzhuang in Zaozhuang City, Shandong.

It sits in the center of the route of the Beijing-Hangzhou Grand Canal. It has three kilometers of ancient waterways and 15 kilometers of waterside streets and lanes, and is known as "the living fossil of the canal culture". The Zaozhuang section of the Beijing-Hangzhou Grand Canal is still an important north-south shipping hub. Photograph by Zhang Weiguo

"端鼓腔"表演。这是一种汉族传统曲艺艺术，发源于微山湖一带，距今已有1000多年的历史，由渔民驱疫降福、喜庆丰收的祭礼仪式演变而来。图 / 陈保成

A Duangu Opera performance. It is a traditional folk art of the Han ethnic group that originated around Weishan Lake in Shandong, with a history of more than 1,000 years. It evolved from the sacrificial rituals of fishermen to drive away epidemics, bring blessings, and celebrate harvests. Photograph by Chen Baocheng

梁山武术表演。济宁市梁山县是"武术之乡"，梁山武术是与少林、武当、峨眉齐名的中华武术四大流派之一。图 / 李继保

A Liangshan martial arts performance. Liangshan County in Jining City, Shandong is a "hometown of martial arts". Liangshan, Shaolin, Wudang, and Emei are known as the four major schools of Chinese martial arts. Photograph by Li Jibao

鲁南皮影戏演出。鲁南皮影戏发源于枣庄，至今已传承百年。图 / 夏晓民

A southern Shandong shadow play performance. This folk art originated in Zaozhuang and has been passed down for nearly a century. Photograph by Xia Xiaomin

鲁南花鼓表演。鲁南花鼓诞生于枣庄市台儿庄，已有 200 余年历史。图 / 孙中喆

A southern Shandong Flower Drum Opera show. This genre, born in Tai'erzhuang, Zaozhuang, has a history of more than 200 years. Photograph by Sun Zhongzhe

河南
云溪燕语卫水舟

5

Henan
Birdsong on the Yunxi Bridge and Boats on the Weihe River

在河南省鹤壁市浚县，古老的卫河（隋朝称为永济渠）蜿蜒曲折，萦绕古城古街，串联古桥古渡，连接历史与现在，昔日的“云溪燕语卫水舟”，依旧“橹桨声声入梦来”。

河南是隋唐大运河的源头和核心区域，是大运河河道路线最长、流经古都最多、运河遗产最为丰富的省份。大运河河南段主要由隋唐大运河通济渠北段、永济渠南段及京杭大运河会通河台前段构成，涉及洛阳、郑州、开封、商丘、焦作、新乡、鹤壁、安阳、濮阳等9个省辖市，以及巩义、永城、滑县3个县（市）。大运河河南段运河文化遗址遗存涵盖了河道、码头、河堤、桥梁、仓窖、水工设施等完整的遗产类型。洛阳市回洛仓遗址和含嘉仓遗址、通济渠郑州段、通济渠商丘南关段、通济渠商丘夏邑段、卫河（永济渠）滑县—浚县段、浚县黎阳仓遗址共7项遗产列入中国大运河世界遗产点段。

大运河河南段拥有以洛阳、开封、商丘等为代表的运河古都文化，以道口镇、朱仙镇等为代表的运河古镇文化，古庙会、海神乐与木版年画等非物质文化遗产。

The ancient Weihe River, called the Yongji Canal in the Sui Dynasty, flows through Xunxian County, Hebi City in central Henan, meandering around the ancient city and its streets, connecting historical bridges and ferries, and linking the past with the present. The city evokes memories of the past when “birds sang on the Yunxi Bridge, and boats sailed on the Weihe River” and “the splash of oars came into dreams”.

Henan was the source and core area of the Grand Canal in the Sui and Tang dynasties. It is also the province with the longest stretch of the Grand Canal, the most ancient capitals, and the richest canal heritage.

The Henan section of the Grand Canal is mainly composed of the northern part of the Tongji Canal and the southern part of the Yongji Canal, and a part of the Huitong River. Here the Grand Canal flows through nine cities (Luoyang, Zhengzhou, Kaifeng, Shangqiu, Jiaozuo, Xinxiang, Hebi, Anyang, and Puyang) and three counties (Gongyi, Yongcheng, and Huaxian).

The canal cultural relics in this section consist of riverways, wharfs, embankments, bridges, granaries, and water conservancy facilities. Seven items from Henan are listed in the World Heritage Site of the Grand Canal, namely, the Huiluo and Hanjia granaries in Luoyang, the Zhengchou section of the Tongji Canal in Zhengzhou, the Nanguan section and the Xiayi section of the Tongji Canal in Shangqiu, and the Huaxian-Xunxian section of the Yongji Canal in Anyang and Hebi, and the Liyang Granary in Hebi.

Henan has many ancient cities, and this section represents the ancient capital culture of the Grand Canal. Foremost among its renowned ancient cities are Luoyang, Kaifeng, and Shangqiu. Henan’s old temple fairs, Sea God music performance, and New Year woodblock prints are part of its intangible cultural heritage.

洛阳，洛河穿城而过。洛河是隋唐大运河通济渠的渠首段。
洛阳是隋唐大运河的中心。图 / 肖社会

The Luohe River passes through Luoyang City, Henan, the center of the Grand Canal in the Sui and Tang dynasties. The Luohe River was the first section of the Tongji Canal in the Sui and Tang dynasties. Photograph by Xiao Shehui

隋唐大运河文化博物馆，坐落于洛阳城区洛河和瀍河交汇处。图 / 徐淑丽

The Sui-Tang Grand Canal Cultural Museum at the intersection of the Luohe and Chanhe rivers in downtown Luoyang, Henan. Photograph by Xu Shuli

隋唐大运河文化博物馆内展出的洛阳运河一号古沉船。这艘明清时期沉船长约 20.14 米，宽 3.48 米，首尾设有生活仓，中部设货仓，是小型内河客货两用运输船。图 / 张健

The wreck of a Ming-Qing boat discovered in the Luoyang section of the Grand Canal, on exhibition at the Sui-Tang Grand Canal Cultural Museum in Luoyang City, Henan.

The boat was approximately 20 meters long and 3 meters wide, with cabins at the front and rear and a warehouse in the middle. It was a small inland-river transport boat used to carry both passengers and cargo. Photograph by Zhang Jian

隋唐洛阳城遗址中的定鼎门。定鼎门是洛阳城中轴线最南端的城门，该处道路和遗址保存完好，发现了大量车辙、人和动物的足迹，这些遗迹为研究古代交通和丝绸之路提供了重要证据。图 / 肖博

The Dingding Gate at the site of Luoyang City in the Sui and Tang dynasties, Henan. It is the southernmost gate on the central axis of the ancient city of Luoyang. The roads and ruins here are well preserved, and a large number of wheel tracks, and human and animal footprints have been found. These relics provide important evidence for the study of ancient transport and the Silk Road. Photograph by Xiao Bo

含嘉仓160号仓窖。含嘉仓是唐代国家粮仓，位于洛阳市，始建于隋朝。含嘉仓遗址总面积约43万平方米，有约400座仓窖。遗址东南角是漕运码头，向东与瀍河、洛河相通。图/戎文文

The No.160 cellar of Hanjia Granary in Luoyang City, Henan. Built in the Sui Dynasty, Hanjia was a state granary in the Tang Dynasty. It had about 400 cellars, with a total area of nearly 430,000 square meters. The wharf on its southeast connects to the Chanhe and Luohe rivers to the east, facilitating the arrival of grain-bearing ships. Photograph by Rong Wenwen

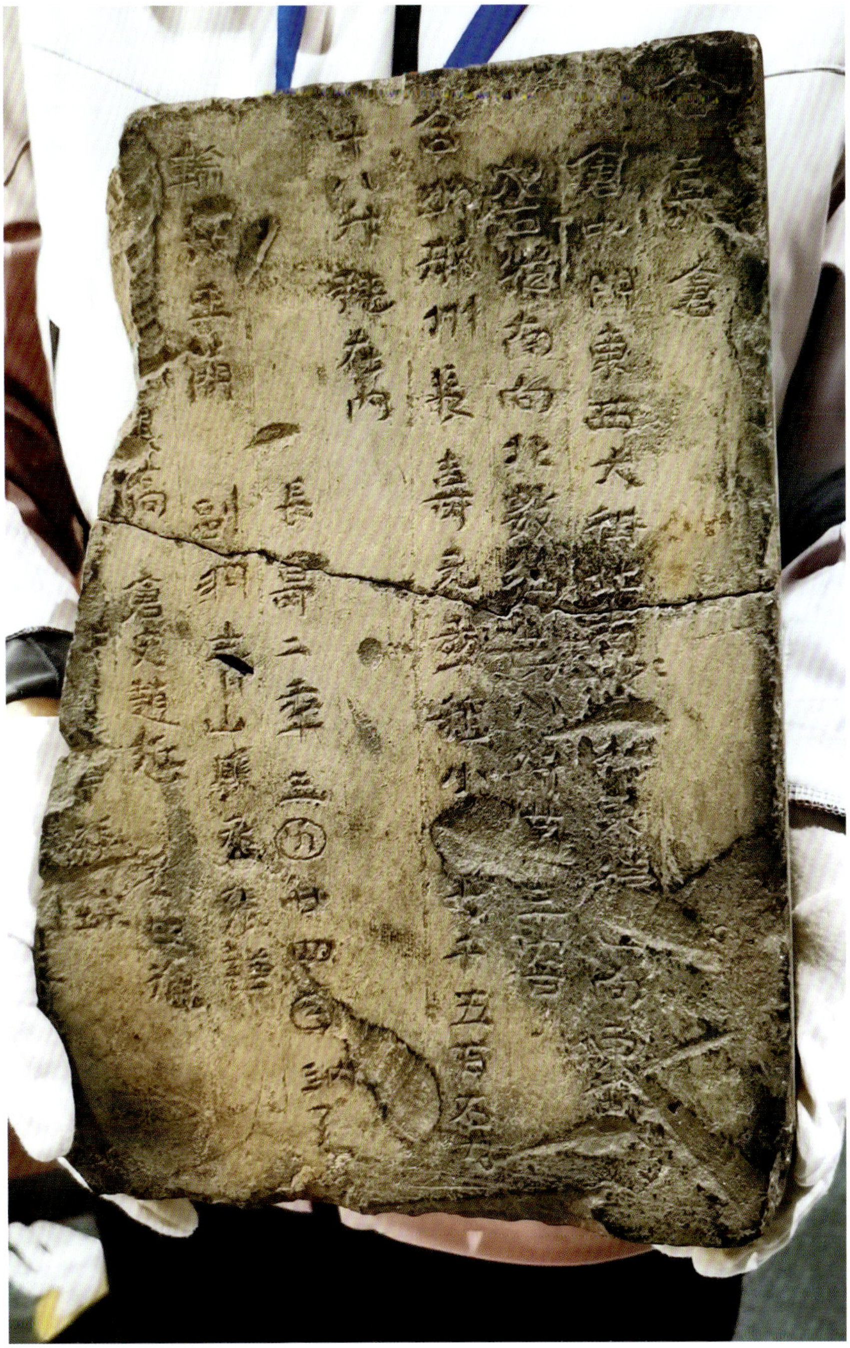

含嘉仓遗址出土的仓窖刻铭砖，记录了仓城名称、仓窖位置、粮食来源地、储粮种类和数量、存入时间、仓窖管理人员等信息。图 / 刘嘉仪

An inscribed brick from the Hanjia Granary. It records the name and location of the granary, where the grain came from, the type and quantity of grain stored, how long it was stored, the management personnel of the granary, and other details. Photograph by Liu Jiayi

洛阳种子博物馆工作人员展示“镇馆之宝”——出土于含嘉仓遗址的“粟”。图 / 黄政伟

A staff member at the Luoyang Seed Museum in Henan displays the museum's “treasure” – millet. The grain was discovered in the ruins of the Hanjia Granary, Luoyang. Photograph by Huang Zhengwei

回洛仓仓窖。回洛仓是国家漕运官仓，位于洛阳，始建于隋朝，是目前中国考古发现仓窖数量最多的古代粮食仓储遗址，有 700 多座仓窖。图 / 成文文

A cellar of the Huiluo Granary in Luoyang City, Henan. Built in the Sui Dynasty, Huiluo was another state granary. Archaeologists discovered more than 700 cellars here, which makes the Huiluo Granary the largest grain storage site in China. Photograph by Cheng Wenwen

郑州，索须河古运河穿城而过。大运河通济渠郑州段包括通济渠索须河段和通济渠惠济桥段。索须河是泄洪排涝河道，其历史可追溯至战国时期。图 / 王安芹

The ancient Suoxu River passes through Zhengzhou City in Henan. The Zhengzhou section of the Tongji Canal includes the Suoxu section and the Huiji Bridge section. The Suoxu River is a flood discharge and drainage channel, whose history can be traced back to the Warring States Period. Photograph by Wang Anqin

惠济桥，桥下是汴河遗址（通济渠在唐宋时期称作汴河），桥上遗留着古代车辙的痕迹。图 / 王安芹

The Huiji Bridge over the remnants of the Bianhe River in Zhengzhou City, Henan. The Tongji Canal was called Bianhe in the Tang and Song dynasties. Traces of ancient wheel tracks can still be seen on the bridge. Photograph by Wang Anqin

卫河蜿蜒穿过安阳市滑县的道口古镇。卫河，开凿于东汉，隋朝称为永济渠，明初改称卫河并沿用至今。图 / 王子瑞

The Weihe River winds through the ancient town of Daokou in Anyang City, Henan. The river, excavated in the Eastern Han Dynasty, was called the Yongji Canal in the Sui Dynasty. It was renamed Weihe in the early Ming Dynasty, and the name has stuck since then. Photograph by Wang Zirui

卫河流经鹤壁市浚县。图 / 程序

The Weihe River flows through Xunxian County, Hebi City, Henan. Photograph by Cheng Xu

黎阳仓遗址，隋唐时期重要的国家官属粮仓，位于浚县。
图 / 王子瑞

The site of the Liyang Granary in Xunxian County, Hebi City, Henan. It was an important state granary in the Sui and Tang dynasties. Photograph by Wang Zirui

浚县古城，建于明朝。卫河从古城外经过，城西门正对着云溪桥。云溪桥是五孔连拱式石桥，也是卫河上仅存的两座古桥梁之一。图 / 李虎

The ancient town of Xunxian in Hebi City, Henan, built in the Ming Dynasty. The Weihe River passes through the town, whose west gate faces the Yunxi Bridge. It is a five-hole stone arch bridge, one of the two remaining ancient bridges on the Weihe. Photograph by Li Hu

通济渠夏邑段遗址展示大厅。图 / 通济渠商丘夏邑段文化遗址展示馆

The exhibition hall at the Xiayi section of the Tongji Canal in Shangqiu City, Henan. Photograph by the Xiayi Section of the Tongji Canal Cultural Relics Exhibition Hall

宋代白釉黑花飞马纹瓷瓶，国家二级文物，出土于通济渠商丘夏邑济阳镇段。通济渠济阳镇段出土大量唐宋瓷器。其器型丰富，窑口齐全，证明了昔日漕运的繁盛。图 / 通济渠商丘夏邑段文化遗址展示馆

A Song Dynasty porcelain vase with white glaze and a pattern of black flowers and a flying horse. It is a national cultural relic, unearthed in the Jiyang section of the Tongji Canal in Xiayi County, Shangqiu City, Henan.

A large number of Tang and Song porcelains were also unearthed in the Jiyang section. The variety of the vessels and the complete kilns prove the prosperity of canal transport in the past. Photograph by the Xiayi Section of the Tongji Canal Cultural Relics Exhibition Hall

通济渠商丘南关段遗址。图 / 魏文慧

The site of the Nanguan section of the Tongji Canal in Shangqiu City, Henan. Photograph by Wei Wenhui

北宋船灯，出土于河南开封州桥及附近汴河遗址。州桥建于唐代，明末被黄河泛滥后的泥沙淤埋。该遗址是2022年度全国十大考古新发现之一。图 / 国家文物局

These Northern Song Dynasty ship lanterns were excavated near the Zhouqiao Bridge and the nearby Bianhe River site in Kaifeng City, Henan. The bridge was built in the Tang Dynasty, and became buried in silt after the Yellow River was in flood in the late Ming Dynasty. This site is one of the top 10 new archaeological discoveries in China in 2022. Photograph by National Cultural Heritage Administration

州桥遗址。图 / 阚力

The site of the Zhouqiao Bridge in Kaifeng City, Henan. Photograph by Kan Li

汴河故道遗迹。图 / 国家文物局

The remains of the ancient course of the Bianhe in Kaifeng City, Henan. Photograph by the National Cultural Heritage Administration

开封铁塔，位于开封市北宋东京城遗址内。塔高 55.88 米，八角 13 层，塔体通砌褐色琉璃砖，似铁柱，元代起民间称其为“铁塔”。遗址内还有繁塔、延庆观等。图 / 易建国

The Iron Tower of Kaifeng at the site of the capital of the Northern Song Dynasty, now part of Kaifeng City, Henan.

The tower is over 55 meters high and has 13 octagonal floors. It is made of brown glazed bricks, which gives it the look of an iron tower, a moniker given to it in the Yuan Dynasty. The Po Pagoda and the Yanqing Temple are also located at the site. Photograph by Yi Jianguo

繁塔，建于北宋，高 36.68 米，有六个面，塔身内外镶嵌 6925 块佛像砖、199 方石刻。图 / 易建国

The Po Pagoda in Kaifeng City, Henan. Built in the Northern Song Dynasty, it is over 36 meters high and has six facades. Inside and outside, the pagoda is inlaid with 6,925 bricks with the Buddha's face on them and 199 stone carvings. Photograph by Yi Jianguo

延庆观的玉皇阁，由青砖、青石和琉璃瓦件砌成。延庆观建于元，与北京的白云观、四川的常道观并称为中国的三大名观。图 / 易建国

The Yanqing Temple in Kaifeng City, Henan. It was built in the Yuan Dynasty. Together with the Baiyun Temple in Beijing and Changdao Temple in Sichuan, it is hailed as one of the three most famous temples of China. The Jade Emperor Pavilion in the temple is made of black brick, limestone, and glazed tiles. Photograph by Yi Jianguo

大相国寺，位于开封州桥遗址东，始建于北齐。图 / 易建国

The Daxiangguo Temple in Kaifeng City, Henan. Built in the Northern Qi Dynasty (550-577) during the Northern Dynasties, it is located east of the Zhouqiao Bridge. Photograph by Yi Jianguo

浚县正月古庙会的民俗表演。该庙会距今已有约 1700 年的历史，从每年农历正月初一持续到二月初二，被誉为“华北第一古庙会”、民俗文化的“活化石”。图 / 柴俊林

A folk performance at the ancient temple fair in Xunxian County, Hebi City, Henan, in the first month of Chinese lunar calendar.

The temple fair has a history of about 1,700 years. Held from the first day of the first lunar month to the second day of the second lunar month every year on the occasion of Chinese Lunar New Year, it has been called the “No.1 ancient temple fair in north China” and a “living fossil” of Chinese folk culture. Photograph by Chai Junlin

道口正月古庙会的民俗表演。庙会于每年农历正月廿七至廿九举行，踩高跷、跑旱船、背阁、抬阁、扭秧歌、武术表演等轮番上演。图 / 王安芹

A folk performance at the ancient temple fair in Daokou Town, Anyang City, Henan.

The fair is held every year from the 27th to 29th day of the first lunar month. Many kinds of acts are performed during the fair, such as stilt walking, boat dance, Yangko dance, and martial arts performances. Photograph by Wang Anqin

洛阳海神乐表演，起源于周朝祭海礼乐，隋唐时期为宫廷宴乐，五代以后流入民间河洛地区，成为求龙降雨的礼乐。演奏团体称海神社。图 / 肖社会

A Sea God music performance in Luoyang City, Henan.

The music originated from the ritual music played while sacrifices were offered to the deities of the sea in the Zhou Dynasty (1046-256 BC). In the Sui and Tang dynasties, it was played during court banquets. After the Five Dynasties (907-960), it spread among the masses in Heluo region centered on Luoyang, turning into ritual music for praying for rain. The troupe is called the Sea God Society. Photograph by Xiao Shehui

工匠们展示开封朱仙镇木版年画的制作。年画题材多取材于民间故事、神话传说、戏曲人物和人们所喜爱与敬仰的英雄豪杰。图 / 易建国

Craftsmen demonstrate how they make New Year woodblock prints in Zhuxian Town, Kaifeng City, Henan. The prints are mostly based on folk stories, myths, and legends about opera characters and heroes. Photograph by Yi Jianguo

6

安徽
濉水清怜红鲤肥

Anhui
The Plump Red Carps Frolicking in the Clear Water of the Suishui River

自古以来，人们逐水而居，城镇因水而兴，商贸因漕运而盛，富庶繁华之地，大多是江河交汇、湖泊相缀。“陴湖绿爱白鸥飞，濉水清怜红鲤肥。”唐代白居易印象中的陴湖、濉水，勾勒出昔日安徽的富庶和美丽。安徽历史上的繁荣兴盛少不了大运河的润泽，这里曾是重要的运河码头、货物集散中心，形成了以柳孜镇为代表的运河重镇，沿河城镇人流如织、商贾云集，码头边桨声楫影，舳舻相继。

大运河安徽段是隋唐大运河通济渠的重要组成部分，流经安徽省淮北、宿州两市。淮北市的柳孜运河遗址和宿州的大运河通济渠泗县段列入中国大运河世界遗产点段。

大运河安徽段文化遗产包括运河故道、桥梁、码头遗址、百善镇百善老街、柳孜古镇等物质文化遗产，淮北花鼓戏、泗州戏、坠子戏、灵璧钟馗画等非物质文化遗产。

Since ancient times, people have lived by water, towns have prospered because of water, and commerce has flourished because of water transport. Most of the prosperous places are those where rivers meet and lakes abound.

"I love the white gulls flying over Pihu Lake and the plump red carps frolicking in the clear water of the Suishui river," wrote Tang Dynasty poet Bai Juyi (772-846), whose poems vividly describe Pihu Lake and the Suishui River and the beauty and prosperity of Anhui in the past.

The prosperity of Anhui in history is inextricably bound up with the prosperity of the Grand Canal. The province used to have a high concentration of wharfs that served as a cargo distribution center. A cluster of towns developed along the river course, chock-a-block with travellers and merchants, and docks full of the splash of oars and the shadow of passing boats.

The Anhui section was an important part of the Grand Canal in the Sui and Tang dynasties, with the canal flowing through two cities, Huaibei and Suzhou. In Huaibei it flows as the Liuzi Canal, and in Suzhou though Sixian County as the Sixian section of the Tongji Canal. Both these sections are included in the World Heritage Site of the Grand Canal.

The cultural heritage of the Anhui section of the Grand Canal includes tangible heritage such as old riverways, bridges, docks, the ancient town of Liuzi, and an old street in Baishan Town. It also has rich intangible heritage such as the Huaibei Flower Drum Opera, the Sizhou Opera, the Zhuizi Opera, and the Zhong Kui folk painting that originated in Lingbi County.

宿州，大运河水穿过村落。大运河通济渠宿州泗县段，现存较完好的运河原始有水故道约 28 公里。图 / 吴天元

The Grand Canal passes through Sixian County in Suzhou City, Anhui. The Sixian section of the Tongji Canal is well-preserved and nearly 28 kilometers long. Photograph by Wu Tianyuan

曹苗考古发掘点，宿州。2012 年，考古部门对泗县境内的曹苗段运河故道进行了考古发掘，出土了一批珍贵文物。图 / 吴天元

The Caomiao archaeological excavation site in Sixian County, Suzhou City, Anhui. In 2012, archaeological departments excavated the old riverway here and unearthed a group of precious cultural relics. Photograph by Wu Tianyuan

古井“十里井”，位于汴河北岸，因距离泗县城十里得名。这口井是运河人家为保障生活用水而挖掘的。旁边村庄亦名为“十里井”。图 / 吴天元

The Shili Well (Ten-Mile Well), an ancient well on the north bank of the Bianhe River in Suzhou City, Anhui. It was named to mark its distance from Sixian County, which was 10 *li*, equivalent to 5 kilometers today. The well was dug by local residents to ensure water for their daily needs. The village nearby is named after the well. Photograph by Wu Tianyuan

隋唐大运河与新濉河交叉口——大运河泗县申遗段最东端。
图 / 吴天元

The intersection of the Sui-Tang Grand Canal and the New Suishui River – the easternmost section of the Grand Canal in Sixian County, Suzhou City, Anhui. Photograph by Wu Tianyuan

淮北市柳孜运河遗址，古代通济渠穿镇而过。这里考古发掘出唐宋时期的河道、河堤、石筑桥墩、道路等重要遗迹，出土 9 艘木质沉船及大批陶瓷器、骨角器、石锚、铜钱等重要文物。图 / 张玲莉

The site of the Liuzi Canal in Huaibei City, Anhui. Archaeologists have excavated important relics here, such as water channels, river embankments, stone piers, and roads from the Tang and Song dynasties. They also found nine wooden shipwrecks and a large number of important cultural relics such as ceramics, bone and horn tools, stone anchors, and copper coins. Photograph by Zhang Lingli

柳孜运河遗址永久性保护大棚建设项目，用于保护展示遗址处的文物古迹。图 / 赵雪华

A permanent shed has been built to protect and exhibit the cultural relics at the site of the Liuzi Canal in Huaibei City, Anhui. Photograph by Zhao Xuehua

淮北市隋唐大运河博物馆珍藏的隋唐时期古沉船。图 / 李博

Ancient shipwrecks from the Sui and Tang dynasties on display at the Sui-Tang Grand Canal Museum in Huaibei City, Anhui. Photograph by Li Bo

隋唐大运河博物馆展出的百善镇隋堤遗址。图 / 周方玲

The ruins of a Sui Dynasty embankment in Baishan Town on display in the Sui-Tang Grand Canal Museum in Huaibei City, Anhui. Photograph by Zhou Fangling

柳孜运河遗址出土的北宋景德镇窑影青釉抱鞠童，国家一级文物。图 / 周方玲

"A Young Child Holding a Ball", a celadon-glazed miniature. This artifact from the Northern Song Dynasty was made in Jingde Town, Jiangxi, the "porcelain capital". It was excavated at the site of the Liuzi Canal and has been classified as a national cultural relic. Photograph by Zhou Fangling

淮北花鼓戏，安徽省地方戏曲之一，具有浓郁的民间特色和演唱风格，发源于淮北地区，表演时男角上场背花鼓，乐队伴奏时也以“花鼓”为主乐。图 / 祖军

The Huaibei Flower Drum Opera, one of the local operas of Anhui, originated in the northern part of the province. It has a strong folk singing style. During the performance, the male actor comes on stage with a flower drum on his back. The flower drum is a type of double-skinned hand drum normally painted red on the sides, and is the main accompaniment for the singing and the dances. Photograph by Zu Jun

泗州戏演员在淮北市隋唐运河古镇景区演出《挡马》曲目。泗州戏发源于宿州市泗县，流行于安徽淮河两岸，距今已有近三百年历史。泗州戏唱腔念白有北方戏曲的激昂慷慨、南方戏曲的温柔舒缓，有难度极大的花腔和花舌及民间琴书的平实质朴。图 / 李鑫

Sizhou Opera actors perform ***Stop the Horse*** in the scenic spot of the Sui-Tang Grand Canal Ancient Town in Huaibei City, Anhui.

The Sizhou Opera originated in Sixian County, Suzhou City, and is popular on both sides of the Huaihe River in Anhui, with a history of nearly 300 years. The singing combines the passion of the northern opera and the soothing gentleness of the southern opera. Technically, it has a highly difficult coloratura, an elaborate passage of music with runs, trills, and wide leaps, but the plot follows the homely simplicity of Qinshu performance (storytelling, mainly with song, usually with the accompaniment of the dulcimer and *erhu*, a two-string fiddle). Photograph by Li Xin

宿州市汴河镇的坠子戏演出。坠子戏是宿州市传统戏剧，因其主要伴奏乐器为坠胡而得名。其吸收京剧、豫剧的一些表演方法，有单唱、对口唱、多人分唱；唱腔流畅婉转，词句通俗易懂，为群众喜闻乐见。图 / 祖军

A Zhuizi Opera show in Bianhe Town, Suzhou City, Anhui.

The Zhuizi Opera, a traditional opera of Suzhou, is named after its main musical instruments, the ***zhuihu***, a two-stringed bowed instrument made of wood, and the ***zhuibang***, a wooden percussion. The genre has absorbed some features of Peking Opera and Henan Opera, including solo singing, duets, and choruses. With its melodious singing and easy-to-follow lyrics, the Zhuizi Opera is a very popular genre in Anhui. Photograph by Zu Jun

“灵璧百人画钟馗”活动在宿州市灵璧县钟馗文化园举办。钟馗画是用于驱邪祈福带有吉祥意味的民俗画。灵璧是“中国民间艺术（钟馗画）之乡”。灵璧第一幅钟馗画传说出自唐朝画圣吴道子之手。作为隋唐大运河的物流节点，宋代有大批钟馗画画家聚集于灵璧，这为灵璧钟馗画诞生提供了艺术土壤。图 / 张启才

A Hundred People Painting Zhong Kui event in the Zhong Kui Cultural Park in Lingbi County, Suzhou City, Anhui.

The Zhong Kui folk painting depicts the feats of Zhong Kui, the demon hunter, who, according to Chinese mythology, vanquished ghosts and other evil beings. The first painting of this genre is attributed to Tang Dynasty artist Wu Daozi (680-759).

Lingbi was a logistics hub on the Grand Canal in the Sui and Tang dynasties. In the Song Dynasty, it was home to a large number of artists specialized in painting Zhong Kui. This provided artistic soil for the birth of this genre of art in Lingbi. Photograph by Zhang Qicai

7

江苏
帆将灯影过扬州

Jiangsu
The Passing Boats Cast Their Light and Shadow on the River Through Yangzhou

“风度钟声来北固，帆将灯影过扬州。”北固的钟声伴随晚风而来，灯光和帆影氤氲在水面上，小船经过繁华的扬州城。古往今来，多少人从这段河道上来往经过，听闻这风声、钟声、船桨击水声？那声音声声入耳，传响了千百年。

大运河江苏段是中国大运河开凿时间最早、流域面积最广、通航里程最长、文化积淀最厚、国家级历史文化名城名镇最多的河段，全长约790公里，流经徐州、宿迁、淮安、扬州、镇江、常州、无锡、苏州8个市，沟通微山湖、骆马湖、洪泽湖、高邮湖及太湖，连接淮河、长江两大水系。江苏段有世界遗产28处，包括中运河宿迁段、淮阳运河淮安段、淮阳运河扬州段、江南运河常州城区段、江南运河无锡城区段、江南运河苏州城区段6处河道以及淮安清江大闸等22个遗产点。

“The evening breeze brings the sound of bells to the Beigu Mountain, and the passing boats cast their light and shadow on the river through Yangzhou.” Down the ages, countless people have passed by this section of the Grand Canal and heard the wind, the bells, and the splash of oars hitting the water, sounds that have been heard for thousands of years.

The Jiangsu section is the earliest constructed section of the Grand Canal, with the largest drainage area, the longest navigable course, the richest cultural heritage, and the largest number of historical and cultural cities and towns. The canal flows through eight cities (Xuzhou, Suqian, Huai’an, Yangzhou, Zhenjiang, Changzhou, Wuxi, and Suzhou) for about 790 kilometers, connecting five lakes (Weishan, Luoma, Hongze, Gaoyou, and Taihu) and linking two rivers (Huaihe and Yangtze). There are 28 World Heritage sites along this section, including six riverways (the Suqian section of the Central Canal, the Huai’an and Yangzhou sections of the Huaiyang Canal, and the Changzhou, Wuxi and Suzhou sections of the Jiangnan Canal) and 22 engineering facilities such as the Qingjiang sluice in Huai’an.

窰灣碼頭

徐州市窑湾古镇码头今貌。大运河徐州段自古是南北航运黄金水道、苏北鲁南水陆枢纽。窑湾古镇，西傍大运河，东临骆马湖，依托水运，逐渐发展成为大运河上的重要码头和商业重镇。明末清初，窑湾漕运达到鼎盛时期，窑湾“口过桅帆千杆，夜泊舟船十里”。图 / 张红

The Yaowan Wharf in the ancient town of Yaowan, Xuzhou City, Jiangsu.

The Xuzhou section of the Grand Canal has been a golden waterway for north-south shipping and a land-water transport hub in northern Jiangsu and southern Shandong since ancient times. Yaowan, with the Grand Canal to its west and Luoma Lake to its east, developed into an important wharf and commercial town, thanks to canal transport. In the late Ming Dynasty and the early Qing Dynasty, the canal transport in Yaowan reached its peak, with “thousands of masts sailing by every day, and boats moored for miles at night”. Photograph by Zhang Hong

船只沿着中运河行经宿迁市宿城区东关口。东关口曾是古代稽查航运、纳税的重地，更是曾经的码头和进出口货物集散地。

宿迁是中国唯一拥有隋唐通济渠、元代黄河故道、清代中运河三个不同历史时期运河主航道的城市。中运河是人工河流。图 / 张红

Ships pass through Dongguankou in Suqian City, Jiangsu.

Suqian is the only city in China that has three canals from different historical periods: the Tongji Canal from the Sui and Tang dynasties, the old course of the Yellow River in the Yuan Dynasty, and the Central Canal in the Qing Dynasty. Dongguankou was an important shipping and taxation inspection site as well as a dock and a cargo distribution center. Photograph by Zhang Hong

中运河宿迁段上的刘老涧船闸。京杭大运河宿迁段全长 112 公里，建有皂河船闸、宿迁船闸、刘老涧船闸、泗阳船闸四座船闸。图 / 刘鑫

The Liulaojian sluice at the Suqian section of the Central Canal in Suqian City, Jiangsu.

This section is 112 kilometers long and has four sluices – Zaohe, Suqian, Liulaojian, and Siyang. Photograph by Liu Xin

龙王庙行宫，坐落于宿迁市皂河古镇运河畔。行宫始建于清朝顺治年间，几经改建，形成占地36亩、四院三进封闭式合院的北方官式建筑群。乾隆皇帝六次下江南，五次驻跸于此，并建亭立碑，故这里又称“乾隆行宫”。图 / 杨青

The Dragon King Temple Palace by the canal in Zaohe, an ancient town in Suqian City, Jiangsu.

The palace was built during Qing Emperor Shunzhi's reign (1644-1661). After several reconstructions, today it is a northern-style complex sprawling over 2.4 hectares, decorated with pavilions and steles. The complex has four enclosed courtyards joined by three entrances along the central axis. It is also called "Emepror Qianlong's Temporary Palace" as the emperor had stayed here five times during his six inspection trips to the south of the Yangtze. Photograph by Yang Qing

大运河淮安段五河口——淮沭河、二河、古黄河、盐河和京杭大运河五条河流交汇处。京杭大运河在淮安境内长达 68 公里，拥有多项“运河之最”：世界上最大的河坝、世界最大的水上立交、中国大运河最古老的航道、中国大运河仅存的保存完好的古闸等。图 / 石浩

Five rivers meet in the Huai'an section of the Grand Canal – the Huaishu River, the Erhe River, the ancient Yellow River, the Yanhe River, and the Beijing-Hangzhou Grand Canal. The Huai'an section is 68 kilometers long, and boasts many firsts: the world's largest river dam, the largest water interchange, the oldest waterway of the Grand Canal, and the only well-preserved ancient sluice of the Grand Canal. Photograph by Shi Hao

里运河文化长廊，贯穿淮安东西，全长 32 公里，包含清口枢纽、清江大闸、淮扬运河淮安段等文化遗产。图 / 李智跃

The Li Canal Cultural Corridor in Huai'an City, Jiangsu.

It runs east to west for 32 kilometers, comprises heritage sites such as the Qingkou hub for canal transport, the Qingjiang sluice, and the Huai'an section of the Huaiyang Canal. Photograph by Li Zhiyue

清江大闸，建于明朝，是京杭大运河上至今唯一保存良好且在使用的大闸。图 / 董海军

The Qingjiang sluice in Huai'an City, Jiangsu.

Built in the Ming Dynasty, it is the only well-preserved sluice still in use along the Beijing-Hangzhou Grand Canal. Photograph by Dong Haijun

总督漕运部院旧址，位于淮安市。其前身总督漕运署是明清时期管理全国漕运的最高机关。图 / 刘洪林

The site of the former Canal Transport Governor's Office in Huai'an City, Jiangsu.

The office was the highest authority in charge of the national canal transport in the Ming and Qing dynasties. Photograph by Liu Honglin

淮安府署，是明清时期淮安府的官署机构，主要职能包括管理地方行政事务、司法审判、财政税收等。图 / 陆明华

The Huai'an Government Office in the Ming and Qing dynasties in Huai'an City, Jiangsu.

Its main functions were managing local administrative affairs, judicial trials, and finance and taxation. Photograph by Lu Minghua

河道总督府（清晏园），位于淮安市，是我国治水史和漕运史上唯一保存完好的总督级别的水利管理衙署园林。图 / 赵启瑞

The Qingyan Garden, or the Riverway Governor's Office, in Huai'an City, Jiangsu.

It is the only well-preserved official garden at the governor's level in the history of water conservancy and canal transport in China. Photograph by Zhao Qirui

清口枢纽的U形河道。清口枢纽位于淮安市大运河、黄河、淮河的交汇之处。图 / 贺敬华

The U-shaped riverway at the Qingkou hub for canal transport in Huai'an City, Jiangsu.

The Qingkou hub is at the intersection of the Grand Canal, the Yellow River, and the Huaihe River in Huai'an. Photograph by He Jinghua

双金闸，位于淮安市清口枢纽遗产区之内，始建于清康熙年间。图 / 董海军

The Shuangjin sluice at the Qingkou hub in Huai'an City, Jiangsu.

The sluice was built during Qing Emperor Kangxi's reign (1661-1722) . Photograph by Dong Haijun

洪泽湖大堤，位于淮安市洪泽湖东岸，始建于东汉，是世界上最长最宽的大堤，有着“水上长城”的美誉。图 / 杨默

The Hongze Lake Dam on the east bank of the lake in Huai'an City, Jiangsu.

Built in the Eastern Han Dynasty, it is the longest and widest dam in the world, dubbed the “Great Wall on water”. Photograph by Yang Mo

板闸遗址，位于淮安市，建于明朝。图 / 董海军

The site of the Ban sluice in Huai'an City, Jiangsu.

It was built in the Ming Dynasty. Photograph by Dong Haijun

古邗沟故道流经扬州市射阳湖镇。邗沟是人工运河，开凿于春秋时期，连接了长江和淮河。大运河扬州段长约 160 公里，有古邗沟故道、高邮明清大运河故道、邵伯明清大运河故道、里运河、扬州古运河、瓜洲运河、瘦西湖等文化遗产。图 / 刘亭

The ancient Hangou Canal flowing through Sheyanghu Town, Yangzhou City, Jiangsu.

Hangou is an artificial canal constructed in the Spring and Autumn Period, connecting the Yangtze and Huaihe rivers. The Yangzhou section of the Grand Canal is about 160 kilometers long, and there are cultural heritage sites along the route such as the ancient riverway of the Hangou Canal, the ancient riverway of the Ming-Qing Grand Canal in Gaoyou, and the ancient riverway of the Ming-Qing Grand Canal in Shaobo, the Li Canal, the ancient Yangzhou Canal, the Guazhou Canal, and the Slender West Lake. Photograph by Liu Ting

运河三湾风景区，位于扬州市。扬州北高南低，水势直泻难蓄，船只经常搁浅。明朝，扬州城一段 100 多米长河道被“舍直改弯”，增加河道长度和曲折度抬高水位、减缓流速，后人称该段河道为“三湾子”。图 / 刘鑫

The Grand Canal Sanwan Scenic Area in Yangzhou City, Jiangsu.

The topography of Yangzhou is high in the north and low in the south, so the water running down was hard to store, and ships often ran aground. To rectify this, three bends were created in the Ming Dynasty, and over 100 meters of the riverway in Yangzhou became curved. This increased the length and tortuosity of the riverway, raised the water level, and slowed down the flow rate. Later, this riverway got its name "Sanwanzi" (meaning "three bends"). Photograph by Liu Xin

瓜洲合江口（大运河与长江的交汇点），位于扬州市。瓜洲是长江与运河交汇处的历史文化名镇，最初为水下暗沙，随江潮涨落时隐时现，晋朝露出水面，逐渐形成渔村、集镇，因形状如瓜而得名。图 / 叶泓

The Guazhou estuary, where the Grand Canal and the Yangtze River meet, is located in Yangzhou City, Jiangsu.

Guazhou (meaning "melon-shaped islet"), a famous historical and cultural town, was originally an underwater shoal, which appeared and disappeared with the rise and fall of the river tide. It finally emerged from the water in the Jin Dynasty and gradually became a fishing village and a market town. Photograph by Ye Hong

高邮市的明清运河故道蜿蜒于城区，环绕镇国寺。明清运河故道（里运河）纵贯高邮南北共 43.6 公里，途经南门大街、镇国寺塔、平津堰等文化遗产。图 / 刘亭

The Zhenguo Temple encircled by the Li Canal in Gaoyou City, Jiangsu.

The Li Canal, the ancient riverway of the Ming-Qing Grand Canal in Gaoyou, runs through the city from north to south with a total length of over 40 kilometers. It passes through several cultural heritage sites such as the Nanmen Street, the Zhenguo Pagoda, and the Pingjin Barrage. Photograph by Liu Ting

新年期间热闹非凡的盂城驿南门大街。盂城驿是全国规模最大、保存最完好的古代驿站，位于高邮市城南历史街区、大运河畔，始建于明朝，有厅房 100 余间。图 / 王林山

The Nanmen Street at the Yucheng Courier Station in Gaoyou City, Jiangsu, during the Spring Festival.

The station is the largest and best-preserved ancient courier station in China with more than 100 halls and rooms. It was built in the Ming Dynasty and lies in the Chengnan Historical Block in southern Gaoyou, beside the Grand Canal. Photograph by Wang Linshan

刘堡减水闸遗址，位于扬州市淮扬运河宝应段东岸，始建于明朝。减水闸用于调节运河与宝应湖之间的水位差，保护大运河堤防安全。图 / 陆明华

The site of the Liubao distributary sluice on the eastern bank of the Baoying section of the Huaiyang Canal in Yangzhou City, Jiangsu.

The sluice was built in the Ming Dynasty to regulate the water level difference between the Grand Canal and Baoying Lake and to protect the Grand Canal embankments. Photograph by Lu Minghua

大运河、长江、淮河交汇之处，坐落着中国历史文化名镇邵伯古镇。古镇因东晋著名政治家、军事家谢安在此筑埭治水而得名，至今保留着完整的邵伯古街和众多明清建筑。图 / 李莉

Shaobo, a famous historical and cultural town, in Yangzhou City, Jiangsu.

It stands at the intersection of the Grand Canal, the Yangtze River, and the Huaihe River. The town got its fame due to Xie An (320-385), a famous statesman and military strategist in the Eastern Jin Dynasty, who built dams here for flood control. The Shaobo Ancient Street and the many Ming and Qing buildings here are still intact. Photograph by Li Li

邵伯古镇历史街区西南侧有一座滚水坝，建于 1952 年 10 月，用于蓄水减压。图 / 李莉

To the southwest of the ancient town of Shaobo is an overflow dam. It was built in 1952 to store water and control downstream river flows. Photograph by Li Li

邵伯“大马头”，被称为“运河第一渡”。邵伯明清大运河故道东堤上，自北向南分布着竹巷口码头、“大马头”、朱家巷码头和庙巷口码头四座古码头，客商在此停靠、进行货物贸易。图 / 李莉

The Big Wharf in Shaobo Town, Yangzhou City, Jiangsu.

The Big Wharf was known as “the No. 1 ferry on the Grand Canal”. On the east bank of the ancient riverway of the Ming-Qing Grand Canal in Shaobo, there are four ancient wharfs where merchants docked and traded their goods. From north to south, they are the Zhuxiangkou Wharf, the Big Wharf, the Zhujiaxiang Wharf, and the Miaoxiangkou Wharf. Photograph by Li Li

邵伯古镇古河堤，始建于宋代。图 / 李莉

The ancient embankment in Shaobo Town, Yangzhou City, Jiangsu. It was built in the Song Dynasty. Photograph by Li Li

天宁寺，扬州最早的佛教庙宇之一。清代皇帝南巡乘船沿运河南下，抵达扬州登陆之处，正是天宁寺行宫外的“御马头”。图 / 孟德龙

The Tianning Temple, one of the earliest Buddhist temples in Yangzhou City, Jiangsu.

When the Qing emperors toured the south of the Yangtze by boat along the Grand Canal, they would land at the Imperial Wharf outside the Tianning Temple. Photograph by Meng Delong

扬州瘦西湖，是大运河扬州段的支流。图 / 周社根

Slender West Lake in Yangzhou City, Jiangsu

It is a tributary of the Yangzhou section of the Grand Canal.
Photograph by Zhou Shegen

卢氏盐商住宅，扬州晚清盐商卢绍绪的豪华住宅，占地面积万余平方米，被誉为“盐商第一楼”。图 / 陈建新

Salt Merchant Lu’s Residence in Yangzhou City, Jiangsu.

This was the luxurious residence of Lu Shaoxu, a salt merchant in the late Qing Dynasty. Covering an area of more than 10,000 square meters, it was known as “the No. 1 salt merchant residence in China”. Photograph by Chen Jianxin

扬州盐宗庙，建于清代，是盐商举行祭祀仪礼的场所。这里供奉着最早煮海盐的始祖夙沙氏、最早的盐商胶鬲、最早的盐官管仲。图 / 陈建新

The Yanzong Temple in Yangzhou City, Jiangsu.

Built in the Qing Dynasty, it was the place where salt merchants held their sacrificial rituals. Enshrined in the temple are the three pioneers of the salt trade: Susha, sea salt maker, Jiao Ge, salt merchant, and Guan Zhong, salt official. Photograph by Chen Jianxin

汪氏盐商住宅，扬州晚清盐商汪鲁门的住宅。图 / 陈建新

Salt Merchant Wang's Residence in Yangzhou City, Jiangsu.

It was the residence of Wang Lumen, a salt merchant in the late Qing Dynasty. Photograph by Chen Jianxin

个园，前宅后院的扬州私家园林，清嘉庆二十三年（1818 年）在明代寿芝园旧址上建成。园主盐商黄至筠生性爱竹，园中植有万竿绿竹，因竹叶形似“个”字，故而得名个园。图 / 陈建新

The Geyuan Garden in Yangzhou City, Jiangsu.

It is a private garden with a house in the front and a yard at the back. Geyuan was built in 1818 in the Qing Dynasty, on the site of the Shouzhi Garden from the Ming Dynasty.

Huang Zhiyun, a salt merchant and the owner of Geyuan, was fascinated by the bamboo, and had 10,000 green bamboos planted in the garden. The garden gets its name from the bamboo leaves, which are shaped like the Chinese character “个” (*ge*). Photograph by Chen Jianxin

虎踞桥，位于镇江市江南运河长江入口处，有超过500 年的历史，明清多次重修。图 / 张元景

The Huju Bridge in Zhenjiang City, Jiangsu.

The bridge is located at the confluence of the Yangtze River and the Jiangnan Canal. With a history of more than 500 years, it was rebuilt many times in the Ming and Qing dynasties. Photograph by Zhang Yuanjing

镇江京口闸遗址，始建于唐代。镇江处于长江与京杭大运河的交汇处，是江南运河的起点。京口闸是江南运河上的第一座闸。 图 / 苏建新

The site of the Jingkou sluice in Zhenjiang City, Jiangsu.

Built in the Tang Dynasty, it was the first sluice on the Jiangnan Canal. The Zhenjiang River, located at the intersection of the Yangtze River and the Grand Canal, is the starting point of the Jiangnan Canal. Photograph by Su Jianxin

江南运河流经常州市。大运河常州段连通长江、太湖，开凿于春秋时期，全长约 45.8 公里。图 / 陈海渊

The Jiangnan Canal flows through Changzhou City, Jiangsu.

The Changzhou section of the Grand Canal, built in the Spring and Autumn Period, is about 46 kilometers long and connects the Yangtze River and the Taihu Lake. Photograph by Chen Haiyuan

大运河穿无锡城而过，并环城一周，勾勒出“龟背城”。图 / 陈跃红

The Grand Canal passes through Wuxi City, Jiangsu, and goes around the city, with its trajectory shaped like a turtle's back. Thus Wuxi got its nickname, “Turtle Back City”. Photograph by Chen Yuehong

清名桥历史文化街区，位于无锡市。街区以古运河为中轴，以清名桥为核心，古桥、古塔、古窑、古坊交相错落，主题博物馆、餐厅等聚合成景，原生态风貌与现代气息相得益彰。图 / 吴洙娟

The Qingmingqiao Historical and Cultural Block in Wuxi City, Jiagsu.

The canal is the central axis of the block, and the Qingming Bridge lies at its heart. The landscape comprises ancient bridges, pagodas, kilns, and lanes as well as modern theme museums and restaurants, with the original environment and the modern elements complementing each other. Photograph by Wu Zhujuan

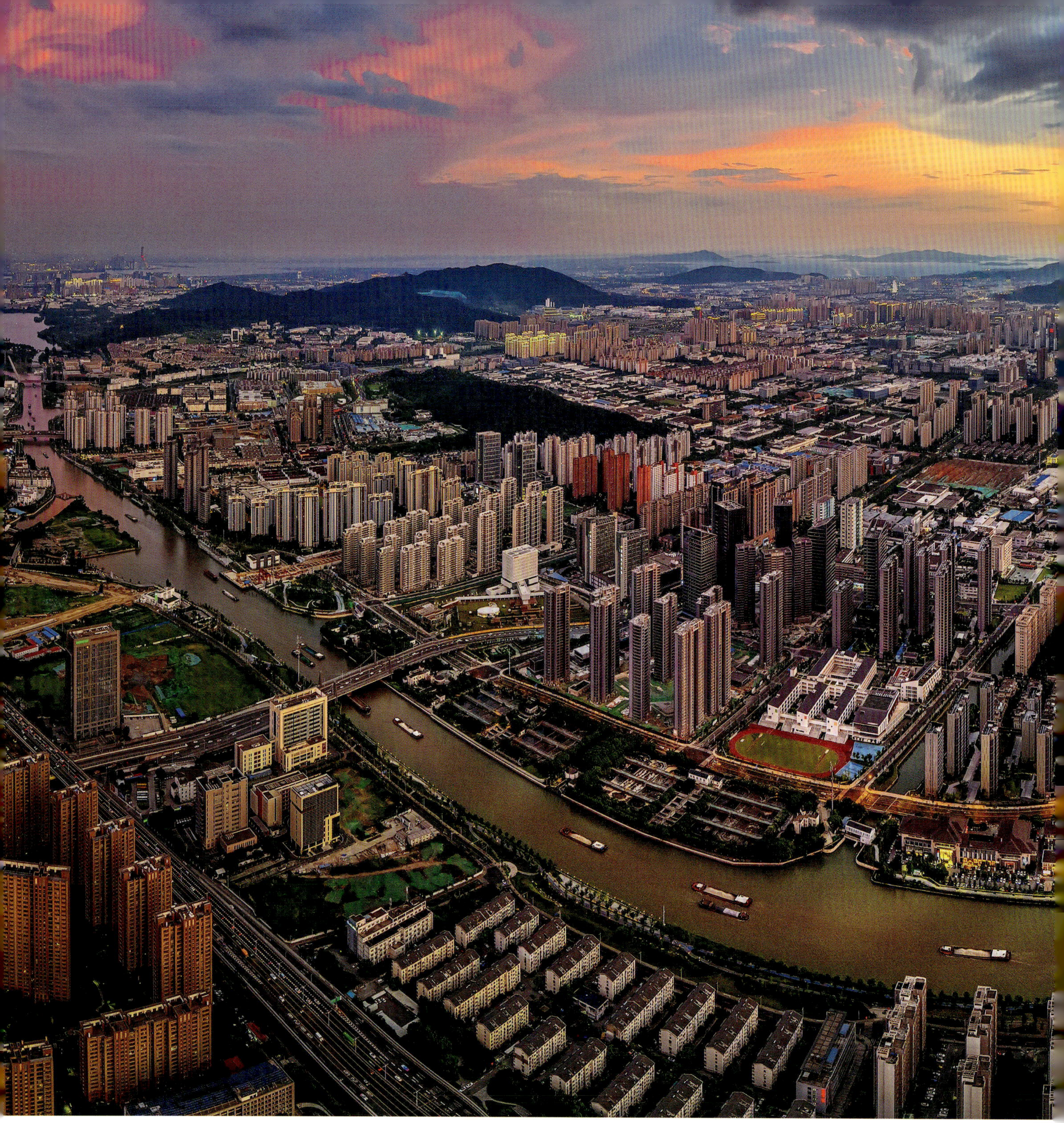

大运河流经苏州城区。苏州是全球首个“世界遗产典范城市”，这里有江南运河苏州城区段运河故道（包括山塘河、上塘河、胥江、环古城河）和盘门、宝带桥、山塘历史文化街区、平江历史文化街区、吴江运河古纤道等文化遗产。图 / 李文学

The Grand Canal flows through Suzhou City, Jiangsu.

Suzhou is the first "world heritage model city" globally. The Suzhou section of the Jiangnan Canal has ancient riverways (including the Shantang River, the Shangtang River, the Xujiang River, and the river around the ancient city) as well as cultural heritage sites such as the Panmen Gate, the Baodai Bridge, the Shantang and Pingjiang historical and cultural blocks, and the Wujiang towpath. Photograph by Li Wenxue

苏州枫桥风景名胜区，以寒山古寺、江枫古桥、铁铃古关、枫桥古镇和古运河“五古”为特色。枫桥横跨古运河上塘河。图／薛祈娟

The Fengqiao Scenic Area in Suzhou City, Jiangsu.

The scenic area comprises five ancient scenic spots: the Hanshan Temple, the Jiangfeng Bridge, the Tieling Pass, the Fengqiao Town, and the canal. The Fengqiao Bridge stands over the Shangtang River. Photograph by Xue Qijuan

万年桥，位于苏州胥门外，跨越城外护城河，建于清代，为三孔石拱桥。
图 / 伊志明

The Wannian Bridge outside the Xumen Gate of Suzhou City, Jiangsu.

Built in the Qing Dynasty, it is a three-hole stone arch bridge straddling the moat of Suzhou. Photograph by Yi Zhiming

山塘河穿越苏州城。唐代白居易任苏州刺史时，对苏州城外西北河道进行疏浚，开挖山塘河，东起阊门渡僧桥，西至虎丘山望山桥，长约 3600 米，称作“七里山塘到虎丘”。图 / 伊志明

The Shantang River runs through Suzhou City, Jiangsu.

The Tang Dynasty governor of Suzhou, Bai Juyi (772-846), had the northwestern riverway outside Suzhou dredged, and the Shantang River excavated. The river stretches from the Duseng Bridge at the Changmen Gate in the east to the Wangshan Bridge in the Huqiu Mountain in the west, about 3,600 meters long. Photograph by Yi Zhiming

苏州山塘历史文化街区夜色。山塘街曾是明清时期中国商贸、文化最为发达的街区之一，被誉为“神州第一古街”。图 / 刘志勇

Night view of the Shantang Historical and Cultural Block in Suzhou City, Jiangsu.

The Shantang Street was one of the most prosperous commercial and cultural streets in China during the Ming and Qing dynasties, and was known as “the No. 1 ancient street in China”. Photograph by Liu Zhiyong

平江历史街区，是苏州迄今保存最完整、规模最大的历史街区，保持着“水陆并行、河街相邻”的格局和“小桥流水、粉墙黛瓦”的江南水城风貌。图 / 王建康

The Pingjiang Historical and Cultural Block in Suzhou City, Jiangsu.

Pingjiang is the best-preserved and largest historical district in Suzhou. It has a parallel land-water layout with the river and the street adjacent to one another, and presents the distinctive landscape of water towns south of the Yangtze with “small bridges, flowing rivers, and whitewashed walls with black tiles”. Photograph by Wang Jiankang

吴门桥，位于苏州古城西南盘门外，跨越古运河（护城河），建于北宋初，清代重修，单孔石拱桥。图 / 毛建军

The Wumen Bridge in Suzhou City, Jiangsu.

The bridge stands over the moat outside the Panmen Gate in the southwest of the old city. It is a single-hole stone arch bridge built in the early Northern Song Dynasty and rebuilt in the Qing Dynasty. Photograph by Mao Jianjun

宝带桥与现代桥梁斜港大桥相映成景。宝带桥横跨苏州澹台湖，全长316.8米，53孔连缀，远观形似一条飘动在河面上的宝带，是大运河沿线现存最长、桥孔最多、结构最轻巧的连拱古石桥。图 / 丁乙

The Baodai Bridge and the modern Xiegang Bridge in Suzhou City, Jiangsu.

The Baodai Bridge spanning Dantai Lake is over 300 meters long and has 53 holes. From a distance, it looks like a precious belt floating on the river. It is the longest multi-arch stone bridge to have survived along the Grand Canal, with the most holes and the lightest structure. Photograph by Ding Yi

吴江古纤道，位于苏州市，始建于唐，重建于元。古纤道是古人行舟背纤的通道。吴江古纤道长约 1800 米，宽 3 米多，是江南运河仅存的一条古纤道。图 / 成林

The ancient Wujiang towpath in Suzhou City, Jiangsu.

Built in the Tang Dynasty and rebuilt in the Yuan Dynasty, it was a passage for people to tow their boats along the bank. The towpath is about 1,800 meters long and more than 3 meters wide. It is the only ancient towpath extant along the Jiangnan Canal. Photograph by Cheng Lin

安德桥，又名平望桥，位于苏州市吴江区平望古镇大运河与頔塘河交汇处，始建于唐。南宋诗人杨万里（1127—1206）曾作诗《过平望》“乱港交穿市，高桥过得桅”，有感桥洞之高。图 / 伊志明

The Ande Bridge (also Pingwang Bridge) in the ancient town of Pingwang, Suzhou City, Jiangsu.

Built in the Tang Dynasty, the bridge is located at the intersection of the Grand Canal and the Ditang River. Yang Wanli (1127-1206), a poet in the Southern Song Dynasty, wrote the poem *Crossing the Pingwang Bridge*, inspired by the height of the bridge: “The chaotic harbor crosses the town, and the high bridge passes the mast.” Photograph by Yi Zhiming

三里桥，位于苏州市吴江区松陵镇的古运河上，始建于元代。三里桥东侧建有纤道。图 / 刘亭

The Sanli Bridge in Songling Town, Suzhou City, Jiangsu.

Built in the Yuan Dynasty, the bridge has a towpath on its east side. Photograph by Liu Ting

8

浙江
吴江水色连堤阔

Zhejiang
The Water of the Wujiang River Laps the Wide Dike

“吴江水色连堤阔，越俗舂声隔岸还。”唐代诗人薛逢（806—874）在《送刘郎中牧杭州》中描绘了杭州附近的自然景观和人文风情。运河滔滔与堤岸相连，水乡人家舂米的声音隔岸传来，江河之水滋养了吴越人家。

大运河浙江段包括江南运河浙江段、浙东运河等河道。江南运河是大运河中形成最早、自然条件最好、连续运用时间最长的河段。浙东运河是春秋时期建成的最早的人工运河之一，是中国大运河南端、海上丝绸之路南起始端，也是中国至今仍在使用和保存最好的运河。在唐代，浙东运河航运地位突出，浙东海上丝绸之路进入较快的发展时期。

大运河浙江段流经嘉兴、湖州、杭州、绍兴和宁波5个市，有江南运河嘉兴—杭州段等5段河道、拱宸桥、水工遗存、古镇集群、历史街区和诗画曲艺等文化遗产。一幅“千年古韵、江南丝路、通江达海、运济天下”的画卷在古代勾勒，在今日着色。

“The water of the Wujiang River laps the wide dike, and the sound of rice pounding in the land of Yue can be heard across the river.” This is how Tang Dynasty poet Xue Feng (806-874) described the picturesque landscape and folk customs near Hangzhou, Zhejiang. The river nourished the ancient kingdoms of Wu and Yue.

The Zhejiang section of the Grand Canal comprises the Zhejiang section of the Jiangnan Canal, the East Zhejiang Canal, and other riverways. The Jiangnan Canal is the earliest section of the Grand Canal with the best natural conditions and in continuous use for the longest time. The East Zhejiang Canal is one of the earliest artificial canals built in the Spring and Autumn Period. It is the southern end of the Grand Canal in China and the southern starting point of the Maritime Silk Road. It is also the best-preserved canal still in use in China. In the Tang Dynasty, the East Zhejiang Canal played an important role in water transport, ushering in a boom period of the Maritime Silk Road in eastern Zhejiang.

The Zhejiang section of the Grand Canal flows through five cities: Jiaxing, Huzhou, Hangzhou, Shaoxing, and Ningbo. It comprises five segments of river course, including the Jiaxing-Hangzhou section of the Jiangnan Canal. This stretch is rich in cultural heritage ranging from ancient bridges, water conservancy sites, clusters of ancient towns, and historical blocks as well as poetry, painting, and folk art. The Zhejiang section is hailed as the millennium-old “Silk Road south of the Yangtze” connecting rivers and seas and prosperous in water transport.

湖州市南浔区双林镇，江南运河重要支流双林塘穿镇而过。双林塘上有三座三孔石拱桥——万元桥、化成桥和万魁桥，被称为“双林三桥”。图 / 张志坤

The Shuanglintang River, an important tributary of the Jiangnan Canal, passes through Shuanglin Town in Huzhou City, Zhejiang. There are three three-hole stone arch bridges on the River – Wanyuan, Huacheng, and Wankui, collectively known as the Three Bridges of Shuanglin. Photograph by Zhang Zhikun

湖州市南浔古镇，京杭大运河、长湖申运河穿镇而过。
图 / 陆志鹏

The Beijing-Hangzhou Grand Canal and the Changhushen Canal pass through Nanxun, an ancient town in Huzhou City, Zhejiang. Photograph by Lu Zhipeng

嘉兴市乌镇，境内河流纵横交织，京杭大运河依镇而过。图 / 柴俊林

The Beijing-Hangzhou Grand Canal passes by Wuzhen, a water town in Jiaxing City, Zhejiang. Photograph by Chai Junlin

长安闸古代水利工程中修复后的长安坝，位于海宁市，始建于唐代。长安闸古代水利工程采用“一坝（长安坝）三闸（上闸、中闸、下闸）两水澳（上澳、下澳）”的复式结构。三个船闸和两个水澳通过抽放水，调整闸室内的水位，确保大船或载货船平稳通过；长安坝则是在平行于船闸的另一条水道上修建的水坝，用于小船或空船通行。图 / 陈海明

The restored Chang'an Dam in Haining City, Zhejiang. Built in the Tang Dynasty, it was part of the ancient Chang'an sluice. The Chang'an sluice has a complex structure with one dam (Chang'an Dam), three sluices, and two water inlets. The water level in the sluice chamber used to be adjusted by pumping water through the sluices and water inlets to ensure smooth passage of large boats or cargo ships. The Chang'an Dam was built on another waterway parallel to the sluice, used for the passage of small boats or empty boats. Photograph by Chen Haiming

长虹桥，位于嘉兴市，横跨京杭大运河，建于明代。明代诗人潘伦在《长虹桥下波潺潺》中描述石桥“虹影卧澄波，登高供远瞻”。图 / 吴云松

The Changhong Bridge in Jiaxing City, Zhejiang. Built in the Ming Dynasty, it spans the Beijing-Hangzhou Grand Canal. Ming Dynasty poet Pan Lun described the stone bridge in his poem: “The reflection of the arch bridge lies on the clear waves like a rainbow. I can behold the distant scenery from this high point.” Photograph by Wu Yunsong

大运河流经杭州市武林门码头、西湖文化广场一带。武林门始建于隋代，是杭州北面的门户。图 / 王平

The Grand Canal flows through the Wulinmen Wharf and the West Lake Cultural Square in Hangzhou City, Zhejiang. Wulinmen, the gateway to northern Hangzhou, was built in the Sui Dynasty. Photograph by Wang Ping

凤山水城门，杭州唯一现存的水上城门，始建于元代，横亘于中河—龙山河之上。这两条河是连续的河段，以凤山水城门为界，北面称中河，南面则称为龙山河。图 / 吴勇韬

The Fengshan Water Gate, the only extant water gate in Hangzhou City, Zhejiang. Built in the Yuan Dynasty, it straddles the Zhonghe and Longshan rivers. These two rivers are continuous, with the water gate as their boundary. The northern part is the Zhonghe, and the southern part the Longshan. Photograph by Wu Yongtao

乾隆御碑与水利通判厅遗址，位于杭州市。御碑记载了清朝乾隆皇帝一次南巡，考察江苏、浙江、安徽三省交纳皇粮情况，仅浙江无积欠，于是立碑嘉奖。御碑北侧为明代水利通判厅遗址。图 / 柏恩惠

The Qianlong Imperial Stele and the site of the Water Conservancy Administration Hall in Hangzhou City, Zhejiang. The Imperial Stele records a tour of Jiangsu, Zhejiang and Anhui by Qing Emperor Qianlong to inspect grain levies. Only Zhejiang had no arrears, so the stele was erected in recognition of that. To the north of the stele is the site of the Ming Dynasty Water Conservancy Administration Hall. Photograph by Bai Enhui

富义仓，清代光绪年间建造的一个国家战略粮食储备仓库。这里当年是杭州百姓最主要的粮食供应地、江南谷米集散地，朝廷贡粮从这里北运。图 / 张闻涛

The Fuyi Granary was a state warehouse for grain reserves built during Qing Emperor Guangxu's reign (1875-1908). In those days, it was the most important grain supply venue for the people of Hangzhou and the grain distribution center in the region south of the Yangtze. From here, the tribute grain of the Qing court was transported to the north. Photograph by Zhang Wentao

广济桥，位于杭州市，始建于明代，全长78.7米，七孔石拱桥。图／徐根柱

The Guangji Bridge in Hangzhou City, Zhejiang. Built in the Ming Dynasty, it is a seven-hole stone arch bridge nearly 79 meters long. Photograph by Xu Genzhu

杭州桥西历史街区，因位于拱宸桥桥西而得名，长约 800 米。街区仍保存着清末民初沿河民居建筑，有大量近现代工业遗存。图 / 王文澜

The Qiaoxi Historical Block in Hangzhou City, Zhejiang. Located to the west of the Gongchen Bridge, it is about 800 meters long. The residential buildings along the canal, built in the late Qing Dynasty and the early Republic of China period, have been well preserved. It also has a large number of modern industrial remnants. Photograph by Wang Wenlan

拱宸桥，杭州古桥中最高最长的石拱桥，始建于明代。图 / 张志坤

The Gongchen Bridge in Hangzhou City, Zhejiang. Built in the Ming Dynasty, it is the tallest and longest stone arch bridge among the ancient bridges of Hangzhou. Photograph by Zhang Zhikun

杭州西兴古镇，浙东古运河起源之地，也是大运河与海上丝绸之路联通的枢纽点，诞生了替过往客商转运货物的“转运行”——过塘行。图 / 沈颖俊

The ancient town of Xixing in Hangzhou City, Zhejiang. It is the origin of the ancient East Zhejiang Canal, and was a hub connecting the Grand Canal and the Maritime Silk Road. It was the birthplace of the Guotang cargo transfer agency for passing merchants. Photograph by Shen Yingjun

西兴过塘行码头。西兴是钱塘江上四大古渡之一。图 / 张跃敏

The Guotang Wharf at the Xixing Ferry in Hangzhou City, Zhejiang. Xixing was one of the four ancient ferries on the Qiantang River. Photograph by Zhang Yuemin

浙东运河绍兴段与绍兴东湖景区。浙东运河西起杭州西兴古镇，流经绍兴，东至宁波，与海上丝绸之路相连。图 / 陈良

The Shaoxing section of the East Zhejiang Canal and the East Lake Scenic Area in Shaoxing City, Zhejiang.

The East Zhejiang Canal starts from the ancient town of Xixing in the west, flows through Shaoxing, and reaches Ningbo in the east. It was connected with the Maritime Silk Road. Photograph by Chen Liang

绍兴八字桥历史街区，航拍。街区内，小桥、流水、人家构成了江南水乡的画面，八字桥、广宁桥和东双桥等点缀其间。图 / 张志坤

An aerial photograph of the Bazi Bridge Historical Block in Shaoxing City, Zhejiang.

The block presents a typical water town scenery south of the Yangtze. The Bazi Bridge, the Guangning Bridge, and the Dongshuang Bridge are located in this block. Photograph by Zhang Zhikun

八字桥，始建于南宋，位于稽山河、断头河、金鉴溇三条河汇合处，两桥相对而斜，状如八字，故得名。图 / 魏国良

The Bazi Bridge in Shaoxing City, Zhejiang. Built in the Southern Song Dynasty, the bridge stands at the confluence of the Jishan, Duantou, and Jinjianlou rivers. It faces another bridge obliquely, forming the Chinese character "八". This is how the Bazi Bridge got its name. Photograph by Wei Guoliang

广宁桥，始建于南宋。桥拱下有纤道。图 / 魏国良

The Guangning Bridge in Shaoxing City, Zhejiang. Built in the Southern Song Dynasty, the bridge has a towpath under its arch. Photograph by Wei Guoliang

昂桑湖古纤道。

古纤道（原名纤道桥）位于浙东运河绍兴段河面上，自东向西穿越绍兴全境，始建于唐代。图 / 周夏平

A towpath on Angsang Lake in Shaoxing City, Zhejiang.

The towpath, located in the Shaoxing section of the East Zhejiang Canal, crosses the city from east to west. It was built in the Tang Dynasty. Photograph by Zhou Xiaping

鉴湖古纤道。图 / 周夏平　　A towpath on the Jianhu Lake in Shaoxing City, Zhejiang. Photograph by Zhou Xiaping

柯桥古纤道。图 / 史春阳　　A towpath of the Keqiao Bridge in Shaoxing City, Zhejiang. Photograph by Shi Chunyang

虞余运河水利航运设施，位于绍兴市，始建于明嘉靖时期，现存明清及1972年重建的水闸及管理用房。图/徐惠芬

The Yuyu Canal water conservancy and shipping facilities in Shaoxing City, Zhejiang. They were built during Ming Emperor Jiajing's reign (1522-1566). The existing sluice and office were rebuilt in the Ming and Qing dynasties and finally in 1972. Photograph by Xu Huifen

曹娥江两岸堰坝遗址中的老坝底堰坝清代遗存，位于绍兴市浙东运河与曹娥江水系沟通连接点，始建于宋，是历史上重要的交通枢纽和货物盘驳点。图 / 徐惠芬

The site of the Laobadi Barrage at the junction of the East Zhejiang Canal and the Cao'e River in Shaoxing City, Zhejiang. Built in the Song Dynasty, it was an important transport hub and cargo transfer point in the Qing Dynasty. Photograph by Xu Huifen

姚江（别名，余姚江）江穿越宁波市。天然河道姚江是浙东运河余姚段的主体。图 / 沈颖俊

The Yaojiang River runs through Ningbo City, Zhejiang. It is a natural river and forms the main body of the Yuyao section of the East Zhejiang Canal. Photograph by Shen Yingjun

浙东运河宁波三江口，甬江、姚江、奉化江三江交汇的地方。三江口是宁波最早的“宁波港”港埠，开埠于清代。图 / 沈颖俊

The Sanjiangkou waterfront of the East Zhejiang Canal in Ningbo City, Zhejiang. It is the intersection of the Yongjiang, Yaojiang and Fenghua rivers. Sanjiangkou is the earliest “Ningbo Port”, opened in the Qing Dynasty. Photograph by Shen Yingjun

庆安会馆，位于宁波三江口东岸，建于清末，是融天后宫与会馆（舶商航工聚会以及航运行业日常办公、议事的重要场所）于一体的古建筑群。图 / 周夏平

The Qing'an Guild Hall on the east bank of Sanjiangkou in Ningbo City, Zhejiang. Built in the late Qing Dynasty, the complex contains the Tianhou Temple and the Guild Hall, an important meeting place of merchants and ship crew. It was also the office for daily administration and deliberation of shipping affairs. Photograph by Zhou Xiaping

“平字”水则碑，位于宁波市，现存的两块碑石分别立于明代和清代。水则碑是古代宁波府各乡调剂水源水位的标尺，视碑上“平”字出没来启闭水闸闸门。图 / 谢娟芬

The “Ping” water regulation steles in Ningbo City, Zhejiang. The two surviving steles were erected in the Ming and Qing dynasties respectively. Water regulation steles served as a ruler for regulating the level of water sources in Ningbo. The sluice gate was opened when the character inscribed on the stele appeared, and closed when it disappeared. The character on the steles, “Ping”, means peace. Photograph by Xie Juanfen

压塞堰遗址。

姚江水利航运设施，位于宁波市，包括压塞堰遗址、小西坝旧址和大西坝旧址。图 / 谢娟芬

The site of the Yasai Barrage in Ningbo City, Zhejiang.

The Yaojiang River water conservancy and shipping facilities in Ningbo City, Zhejiang. They include the site of the Yasai Barrage, the Small West Dike, and the Big West Dike. Photograph by Xie Juanfen

小西坝、大西坝旧址（图下方建筑设施）隔姚江相望。两坝均建于南宋，如今古坝已无存，仅存的老闸建于 20 世纪 60 年代。图 / 谢娟芬

The sites of the Small West Dike and Big West Dike (bottom) face each other across the Yaojiang River in Ningbo City, Zhejiang. Both dams were built in the Southern Song Dynasty. Today, the ancient dams have vanished and only an old sluice, built in the 1960s, is left. Photograph by Xie Juanfen